DEVELOPING A SECRET HISTORY WITH GOD

MARGARET M. BASS

To Theresa,

God bless you
as you press into
His Presence.

Jeremiah 18:2.

DEVELOPING A SECRET HISTORY
WITH GOD

Margaret J Bass

Rhema Publications
145-157 St John Street – London EC1V 4PW

DEVELOPING A SECRET HISTORY WITH GOD

ISBN 978-0-9568487-7-2

First Published in Great Britain in 2012 by
Rhema Publications Ltd,
Suite 15572 - Lower Ground Floor
145-157 St John Street – London EC1V 4PW

Printed in Great Britain

DEDICATION

To the loving memory of my maternal grandmother,
Annie Reynolds, who made such a loving and spiritual
impact on my early childhood.

Margaret with Grandmother

TABLE OF CONTENT

DEVELOPING A SECRET HISTORY WITH GOD

Through journalizing
As we commune with Him in the Holy of Holies
Where He will feed us Hidden Manna

FOREWORD

In this book I am writing about a hidden fellowship and conversation with God, since, as we develop an intimate relationship with Him, we ultimately cultivate a deep, healthy spiritual root structure in the True Vine. The purpose of this precious prayer time is to mature us, change our hearts, transform our thinking and mold us to His image. It is a daily divine appointment to visit the Potter's house as Jeremiah the prophet wrote: *"arise, and go down to the potter's house, and there I will cause thee to hear my words. Then I went down to the potter's house, and, behold, he wrought a work on the wheels. And the vessel that he made of clay was marred in the hand of the potter: so he made it again another vessel, as seemed good to the potter to make it"* *(Jeremiah 18:2-4).*

We are promised "My sheep hear My voice…" yet many wonder why they do not hear His Voice. So the purpose of this book is to answer many questions too:

- How do we hear and recognize His voice above other voices out there?
- He is calling you today just as He did in the Garden, "Child, where are you?"
- What excuses do we use to justify neglecting this quiet quality time alone with God?
- How do we get to this place of WANTING TO rather than HAVING TO spend time with God?
- How do we overcome the struggles?

God is more interested in what we are BECOMING even more than what we are DOING.

We need to invest in the 'BECOMING' and the 'DOING' will glorify God.

We need to invest in the ROOT STRUCTURE and the HARVEST will bring glory to God.

THIS BOOK WILL BE A LIFE CHANGING EXPERIENCE AND REVOLUTIONIZE YOUR QUIET TIME WITH GOD.

PREFACE

I was born in Aberdeen, Scotland and was raised in Belfast, Northern Ireland. I was the eldest of the eleven children of the Mearns family. I met my husband, John, while we both were serving in the Royal Air Force in England. We have been married for 47 years, and God blessed us with three beautiful daughters who dedicated their lives to spreading the gospel through music, since Kathleen the youngest was 8 and her twin sisters, Patsy and Angela were 12. The girls recorded 6 record albums with several national hit songs on the Christian music charts.

But the year 1972 had seen our family at their lowest, with the pressure a life of emigration brings: with a marriage being pulled asunder and illnesses, but the year 1973 also saw our family rise to the potential God intends, as we surrendered our lives and future to God. We saw our marriage restored, my body miraculously healed, and the ground work was being laid for the future ministry God would call our daughters to, as they were now being brought up in the fear and admonition of the Lord. I have spent most of my married life as a full time homemaker and mother. For ten years the whole family traveled as an evangelistic team sharing the goodness of God through song, the Word and testimony, keeping a schedule of approximately 100 dates per year.

Now that the girls have grown up, God has multiplied our family ministry. The girls continue to minister for the Lord. Angela and her husband, Jeff Buchanan, travel and work for the ministry 'Exodus' located in Orlando, Florida. Kathleen and her husband David Estes, a pastor, are in full time ministry at a church in Northern Virginia just outside Washington D.C. Patsy lives in Nashville Tennessee, teaches and leads worship in her home church, serves in a prison ministry and travels part-time to minister in Nepal and India. I have been teaching at my home church, continuing my freelance writing and traveling to minister the Word through any door that God opens.

Many years ago the girls all left home together to take their gospel music ministry to Nashville Tennessee, which was about 850 miles from our home in Pennsylvania. Talk about instant empty nest syndrome! The fact that our extended family all lived 3000 miles away in Belfast, Northern Ireland, did not help the loneliness. Having been a full time mother meant I did not have a career to turn to for fulfillment. Our fulfillment had been in our family ministry which took up most of our time and energy. Seeing this come to an end added to the loneliness and emptiness. At the same time our local church fell apart due to leadership indiscretions, leaving us without a home church when we needed the fellowship the most.

I never felt so much like I had just been dropped alone in a desert. But only in a desert situation do we have a thirst so desperate that water is a matter of life and death. In my unquenchable thirst God met me in an oasis I had been searching for all my Christian life. I had lived most of my life with a personal relationship to Christ, and was traveling and ministering as a family, and raising our young daughters up in the fear and admonition of the Lord. Although I had been a faithful student of the Word and prayed every day, there was something more my soul was thirsty for. That something I found, by God's grace and mercy, was the realization that He wanted to fellowship with me and that I could converse with Him. He hadn't led me to the desert to abandon me, but rather He had brought me to the desert to meet with me. My life had been so filled and busy doing good things and ministry that God had to bring me to this point of utter aloneness to get my attention. How easy and subtle it is for even a ministry to take the place of God in our lives, using up all our time, attention and priority. It can happen even without you realizing it. By no means am I saying that being in ministry is not serving God. But what I am saying is that it shouldn't pull us away from investing time alone with Him. So often our joy comes from introducing others to Christ and yet investing little time or effort in getting to know the Christ we are introducing others to. I hope you get my point. Of course it brings joy and fulfillment to follow a calling, and see others touched by the message we bring, but it shouldn't be at the expense of neglecting our growth, which comes from intimate time with Him alone.

As I state often throughout this book, God is more interested in what we are becoming even more than what we are doing. We become as we present ourselves as living sacrifices at the potter's house, where He can mold us. When we become what He wants us to be, then we will instinctively do what He wants us to do. Burn out often comes when we try to do things in order to become. Burn out is often a result of sweat from trying to do that which He has not called us to do, or trying to do it with our own strength; but it is *not by might, nor by power, but by my spirit, saith the Lord of hosts (Zechariah 4:6).*

In my utter loneliness I even questioned myself, "Have I been fervently studying the Word just to teach it, or am I searching the Word to find God?" Since then I find it hard to teach a principle that hasn't personally impacted my life. It's amazing how you talk to yourself and search yourself, when God strips away all activity and companionship so that you have no other option than to get to know yourself through the eyes of the One who knows you the most.

I call to remembrance my song in the night; I commune with mine own heart and my spirit made diligent search (Psalm 77:6).

During those years, with nowhere else to turn, I developed an intimate relationship with God that revolutionized my Christian walk. Through this relationship I developed a secret history with God, a root structure that has seen me still standing, even when the tide of life turned against me in an unrelenting way in all areas of my life.

It was the year 2005, the year following our 40th wedding anniversary, when my life took a sharp turn. Charles Dickens said it so well in the opening phrase from his book *A Tale of Two Cities*: "it was the best of times, it was the worst of times."[1]

As a foreign storm from the past blew with gale force winds over the branches of my life it left in its wake a broken heart filled with despair and confusion. A physical body being affected by an emotional wreck of a person from a nervous breakdown and clinical depression causing a broken spirit that could only cry out in despair, "Oh God help me!" However the gathering storms hadn't finished their impact yet, they seemed to be accumulating from the north, south, east and west until a tsunami submerged my whole being, body, soul and spirit and almost drowned me, with the spirit within me rising up to gasp for breath. It seemed to have touched every area of life. When the Word tells us: *keep thy heart with all diligence; for out of it are the issues of life (Proverbs 4:23).* I believe

---

[1] Charles Dickens, *A Tale of Two Cities*, 1859.

it is a warning to us to protect our root structure, our innermost being, since that is the source of all areas of our lives as believers.

Personal emotional hurts and betrayals from my marriage and my childhood drowned me in such waves of pain that at times I could hardly breathe. Due to the clinical depression I had fallen into, I was prescribed an antidepressant, which eventually affected my eyesight so badly that I had to have five immediate eye surgeries. With God's help I weaned myself off the antidepressants just in time to face my next physical battle. Skin cancer so severe I almost lost half of my nose. Not a good scenario for a woman who was trying to regain confidence in her femininity and self as a woman. The stitches were barely out when I was diagnosed with an irregular high heartbeat known as Atrial Fibrillation. I had three cardio versions, during which the surgeon stops the heart and tries to shock it back into rhythm, but all efforts failed. Eventually, in April of 2010, I had to undergo a seven-hour cardiac ablation heart surgery. Unfortunately during the next two evenings my heart went back into Atrial Fibrillation due to fluid on the heart. I was prescribed a strong medication to help it stay in rhythm. During the next several weeks I was continually in the emergency room of my local hospital. After much investigation it was discovered that the medication had poisoned my liver. I just wept, "Oh God will this ever end?" I was told the medication would be in my system for at least one year and although the symptoms would gradually decrease, I would have to live with it until it was totally out of my system. During that year I also had to undergo shoulder surgery leaving me almost dependent on narcotic pain killers. There was still much emotional anguish and uncertainty within my marriage. There were six deaths within the immediate family just one after the other; one was my younger brother's unexpected death. How can I possibly condense this tsunami to a mere paragraph? At the end of the year my doctor told me that if we hadn't found the root of the problem I would have had liver failure within a month and within one more month I would have been dead. God spared my life for a purpose and I believe part of that purpose was to get the message of this book published.

However this tsunami is not the topic of the book. But I wanted to show you my vulnerability by allowing you to see into my heart where God dwells by faith and exposing you to how much I have needed His grace in my life. How much His grace has sustained me, lifted me out of shame, hopelessness and despair and has matured me. I wanted you to know that I am a person who walks with spiritual and emotional limps. And without a healthy root structure developed through a secret history with God my limps would have totally crippled me for life. If I can make it with Him, so can you.

Through those years on an emotional and physical roller coaster a regression had begun in my heart. Trials and circumstances had carried me away from the secure intimacy a child has with a Papa. I felt I had disappointed my heavenly Papa with my reactions to the emotional hurts and betrayals and I could no longer claim that confidence in my intimate relationship to Him, so I shied away. As I crouched in my spiritual corner I clothed myself with shame because I felt the betrayals had stripped me naked. I fed myself with morsels of self pity and injustice just to survive.

I timidly peaked out of my spiritual window to find 'Papa' was in the distance and had suddenly become 'Father' and an authoritative formal figure expecting more from me than I could give. During those times all I could cry out was, "Father, remember that I am only dust!" With this shift in my soul my excitement and childlike wonder of spending time with Papa evaporated leaving only a cloud of spiritual and emotional depression.

As the regression progressed I found myself spiritually hanging by a thread to an almost unreachable God. I questioned why God now seemed so distant, but guess what, God had not moved, rather it was me who had distanced myself from the warmth of His presence and replaced it with the coldness of the reality of the circumstances. I had bought the enemy's lies that it was now hopeless to find my way back to Papa's heart and fulfill my purpose by continuing to follow my calling. I know I cannot confine the Almighty Omnipresent, Omniscient, Omnipotent God to titles like Papa, Father or just God. But I am trying to use these titles to describe the regression of my heart and the alienation I felt as I withdrew myself from those intimate precious times with Him.

The path to that precious time with Papa had been tread down for so many years, that I knew I would eventually find my way back again by following the now overgrown path I had tread before. It was now overgrown with weeds of despair, hopelessness, lack of motivation and most of all discouragement. In my spirit I knew that my discouragement was the devil's calling card! In Dante's work "Inferno" the sign above the entrance to Hades reads: "abandon all hope, ye who enter here." That is why to live in hopelessness is such torture to the soul for it is like experiencing a piece of hell here on earth.

The enemy scoffingly questioned my mind, "How could you encourage others to seek this intimacy with Papa that you once experienced if you have now progressed to this distant relationship? Does this potential book that has laid on your desk for over five years have any authenticity now?" Then I remembered the words my daughter, Kathleen, spoke to me many times through all the emotional drama, physical ailments and surgeries: "Mom, you are still standing!" I was immediately reminded of all the years I had invested in my spiritual root structure. And when the storms began to subside and the dust settled, because my root structure in the True Vine was deep, I was still standing by the grace of God.

"I am made by God, thanks be to Him, such that your misery toucheth me not, nor doth the flame of this burning assail me," from Dante's "Inferno."[2]

God used a song by Josh Groban as a window to my soul during those dark days to lift me up:

> When I am down and, oh my soul so weary;
> When troubles come and my heart burdened be;
> Then, I am still and wait here in silence,
> Until you come and sit awhile with me.
> You raise me up, so I can stand on mountains;
> You raise me up, to walk on stormy seas;
> I am strong, when I am on your shoulders;
> You raise me up to more than I can be.[3]

➢ Was it a testing?

➢ Was it a trial?

➢ Was it a pruning?

➢ Was it the enemy trying to stop or buffet me?

➢ Or was it just the result of living in a fallen world?

It was probably a little of all the above but all used for His glory. I don't know the source BUT I do know the victory and growth.

When the tsunami hit my life was shaken. Did branches of my life break off? Are you kidding? I was reduced to ground level! But when it subsided the root was still stable and full of life because of the years I had invested in the root structure by

---

[2] Dante, "Inferno" Canto 3 Line 9, 14th century epic poem.
[3] "You Raised Me Up" by Secret Garden, by R. Loveland & B. Graham.

developing a secret history with God. I was still deeply rooted in the True Vine. As I watched the leaves gradually falling from my spiritual life like a day in autumn and lying in a pile beneath my feet I asked the Lord:

But, Papa, what are these leaves that are falling from my life grounded in you?

He replied:

Dear Child,
If you do not water, nourish and consistently protect your root structure, the leaves that begin to fall are the leaves of faith, followed by dried up leaves of hope, and the discolored leaves of obedience! Without leaves, which nourish a plant, there will never be fruition of your destiny. A plant without leaves will never blossom and bear fruit. Feed and water your root structure daily and consistently that healthy leaves of faith, hope and obedience in due season, will reap the abundant fruit of your destiny. Do not let the garden of your life of faith be covered by fallen dried up leaves of lost opportunity, lost time and lost potential.
A warning from Papa!

Through His faithfulness I was still standing although many branches had been broken off and those left were pretty bare of leaves but were now beginning to flourish again. Winter is past and I am now sowing again trusting God for a fruitful harvest. This poem from a Hallmark card to encourage me says it so well:

A mighty wind blew night and day, it stole the oak tree's leaves away,

Then snapped its boughs and pulled its bark until the oak was tired and stark.
But still the oak tree held its ground while other trees fell all around...
The weary wind gave up and spoke, "How can you still be standing, Oak?"
The oak tree said, "I know that you can break each branch of mine in two,
Carry every leaf away, shake my limbs, and make me sway.
But I have roots stretched in the earth, growing stronger since my birth.
You'll never touch them for you see, they are the deepest part of me.
Until today, I wasn't sure of just how much I could endure.
But now I've found, with thanks to you, I'm stronger than I ever knew.[4]

Yes, it was certainly as Dickens wrote in *A Tale of Two Cities*: "it was the best of times, it was the worst of times." The hurt, the uncertainty, the hopelessness and despair were the worst of times, but the growth of faith, the maturity and the victories were the best of times. I experienced that, *truly all things work together for good to those who love God and are called according to His purpose (Romans 8:28).*

This life changing message is based not only on Bible study, years of developing my secret history with God, but also drawn from experiences of my own life where the rubber meets the road. Even though I have been a student and teacher of the Word for over forty years, I still feel like a child trying to swim in the deep end, as I venture to write and encourage others on such a deep topic in a simple, relevant way.

This book is a legacy of my walk of faith tried by fire. When the storms began to blow over my life almost six years ago, I had almost completed this book. It had been lying on my desk all these years as if buried under the avalanche of the aftershocks. As the

---

[4] Johnny Ray Ryder Jr., "The Oak Tree."

storms began to subside and the clouds began to disperse the Lord admonished me with these few words:

> *Dear Child,*
> *The seeds I have given you in your writings will only reproduce and give an abundant harvest if they are sown into the field of the world and not just stored in pages on your shelf.*

May my testimony encourage you to develop your own Secret History with God.

INTRODUCTION

This is the generation of them that seek him,
that seek thy face, as Jacob (Psalm 24:6).

Many may question the reason for this book at this time. We are living in a day when we put so much emphasis on our physical well being, by exercising our muscles, and taking extra care of what we eat while feeding our emotional being with motivational material. But may I suggest that many of us are suffering from spiritual malnutrition because we are ignoring Matthew 4:4! It is written: *Man shall not live on bread alone, but on every word that comes from the mouth of God (Matthew 4:4).*

When was the last time you really fed on, chewed over, swallowed and digested the written Word, until it became part of the very sinews of your spiritual being? When was the last time you actually memorized a verse of scripture that you may hide it in your heart? When was the last time you fed upon a personal word from God as you invested the time to not only talk to Him but also to listen in anticipation to hear from Him?

I believe that as the Body of Christ, we are falling into apathy. We lack spiritual vitality to engage the enemy and we have watered down the convictions of our Godly values due to spiritual malnutrition by ignoring Matthew 4:4. My heart's desire for this book is to restore Altars in the House of the Lord. The Bible tells us that we are now the Temple of the Lord, so the Altars that I want to restore are the Altars in our hearts where God will commune with us and feed us His word that we might be spiritually motivated, strong and healthy.

The Bible warns us that in the last days the love of many shall wax cold. Maybe your love of God hasn't waxed cold BUT has it become lukewarm! In Revelations 3:14-22 we read of the church of Laodicea, a type of church in the last days. This church was luke-warm because they had neglected to spend time with God. Their material wealth had caused them to become not only self-sufficient but spiritually blind to their need of time alone with God. To this same church The Lord invites: *behold, I stand at the door, and knock: if any man hear my voice, and open the door, I will come in to him, and will sup with him, and he with me (Revelation 3:20).* This is often used as a salva-tion verse to lead unbelievers to accept the Lord's invitation, but in fact it is an invitation to the church. Has your love grown lukewarm because you have begun to take this salvation for granted? Another sign of the last days is our unthankfulness according to 2 Timothy 3:2. May we stop and count our blessings that once again we may be a thankful people, which will ignite a passionate love for God, and 'a wanting to' not 'a having to' spend time alone with Him.

Or perhaps you are on fire and busy about the Kingdom, BUT you spend so much time ministering to others in the Outer Court that you neglect to press in and spend time ministering to God in the Holy Place. Are you like the church at Ephesus? God was aware of all their labor of love for Him, and yet He still had something against them: they had left their First Love (Revelation 2:4). Our redemption bought back that which was lost in the Garden of Eden – our privilege of intimate fellowship with God! Are we hiding in the Outer Court when God is calling to us "Where are you?" Will our response be, "God, I don't have time to spend with You today BUT I am doing all this ministering for You!" All the while God is beckoning "Child, come apart and spend some time with Me." Understand that God is more interested in what we are becoming than what we are doing! We do not become by doing, we only become as we spend time alone with Him where He can mold us to His image as we behold Him. Then our doing will flow from the becoming and not from the sweat of our own efforts.

The Spirit is drawing us to the Altar of Incense where we may experience an intimate relationship with the Lord.

Draw me, we will run after thee: the king hath brought me into his chambers: we will be glad and rejoice in thee, we will remember thy love more than wine: the upright love thee (The Song of Solomon 1:4).

No man can come to me, except the Father which hath sent me draw him: and I will raise him up at the last day (John 6:44).

Note that we are not DRIVEN but rather we are DRAWN by His love for us!

The Lord hath appeared of old unto me, saying, Yea, I have loved thee with an everlasting love: therefore with loving-kindness have I drawn thee (Jeremiah 31:3).

It is our choice to respond to run after Him.

These are they which were not defiled with women; for they are virgins. These are they which follow the Lamb whithersoever he goes; these were redeemed from among men, being the first fruits unto God and to the Lamb (Psalm 63:8).

My soul follows hard after thee: thy right hand upholds me (Revelation 14:4).

If we run after Him and seek Him with all our hearts He will bring us into His chambers i.e. the Holy of Holies!

> *Dear Child,*
> *Stressful and perilous times are coming on this earth. It will get worse and worse as you see the end coming. That is why My people must strengthen their root structure today, that they will not fall away as the heat of trials is turned up in these last days. Your root structure is your life source to Me, for I am the True Vine. It is essential if you are to survive the days that are coming on the earth. Develop and strengthen this root structure while it is still day!*
> *A warning from Papa!*

For then shall be great tribulation, such as was not since the beginning of the world to this time, no, nor ever shall be (Matthew 24:21).

This know also, that in the last days perilous times shall come (2 Timothy 3:1).

Even if you have not considered that we are living in the last days that the Bible warns us about as believers, we will still have to survive testings and trials in our own personal lives. Generations of saints since the Book of Acts have had to endure tribulations and persecutions, and as saints, we are not exempt. How will we survive the heat of those trials if we have no root structure?

> *Yet hath he not root in himself, but dureth for a while: for when tribulation or persecution ariseth because of the word, by and by he is offended (Matthew 13:21).*

This is not a book about overcoming trials; however it is a book to exhort believers to develop a secret history with God, by spending time alone with Him, that we might have deep roots to survive those trials and live a victorious walk in the world. Because, saints, we can rejoice, for we are promised, in *all these things we are more than conquerors through him that loved us (Romans 8:37).* God has a purpose in mind for those trials: *that the trial of your faith, being much more precious than of gold that perisheth, though it be tried with fire, might be found unto praise and honour and glory at the appearing of Jesus Christ (1 Peter 1:7).* Through those trials we will grow and be conformed to His image (see chapter "Changed from Glory to Glory").

During my service in the Royal Air Force I realized the importance of training in anticipation of war. The military do not wait until the heat of the battle to train and equip their soldiers. As soldiers in the Lord's army we must train now for the battles ahead.

As stated by Watchman Nee: why should we await the Lord's return in passive contemplation? It is spiritual fitness which makes us ready for His coming, and that demands an onward progress with Him now.[5]

Our root structure is our hidden spiritual life, which no one sees, and is developed as we invest time alone with the Father where He will fellowship with us and feed us hidden manna (see chapter "Hidden Manna").

> *He that hath an ear, let him hear what the Spirit saith unto the churches; To him that overcomes will I give to eat of the hidden manna (Revelation 2:17).*
>
> *Behold, I stand at the door, and knock: if any man hear my voice, and open the door, I will come in to him, and will sup with him, and he with me (Revelation 3:20).*

---

[5] Watchman Nee, "Song of Songs," Part 5, Mature Love, CLC publications, 2006, p. 9.

CHAPTER ONE

A SECRET HISTORY WITH GOD

*But thou, when thou pray, enter into thy closet, and when thou
hast shut thy door, pray to thy Father which is in secret;
and thy Father which seeth in secret shall reward thee openly
(Matthew 6:6).*

My secret history with God is the cultivation of my relationship with God as I invest precious time alone with Him, intimate moments that no one else is aware of. In this secret place, hidden from the view of man, the roots of my relationship with and faith in God are nourished, strengthened and deepened. I am not writing about deep Biblical knowledge, rather I want to encourage a deep relationship with God. "Within our hearts is a longing and a profound cry of the soul for something our theologies can only point us to, yet never replace, AN INTIMACY WITH GOD,"[6] writes Ken Gire.

In the parable of the sower Jesus teaches us about the importance of developing a deep root structure.

Some fell upon stony places, where they had not much earth: and forthwith they sprung up, because they had no deepness of earth. And when the sun was up, they were scorched; and because they had no root, they withered away (Matthew 13:5 -6).

---

[6] Ken Gire, *Windows of the Soul*, Zondervan, 1996, flap of the book.

Since the roots of a plant grow beneath the soil where they are invisible to the eye, they are an analogy of our hidden spiritual life, while the leaves and blossom of a plant are the manifested fruit of our spiritual lives. The trouble with much of our walk is that although it might appear there is apparent life above the soil, but under the surface, if our roots were ever exposed there would be very little secret life.

Jesus is warning here of a shallow spiritual life. Our lives today are miserably shallow, especially when compared to believers in other parts of the globe, where many are being persecuted, some even laying down their lives for their faith. If one day we are faced with the option of renouncing our faith or losing our lives, which will we choose? It is not on that day the issue will be settled but rather it is now - today! If we fail Him on that day it will be because we have not sent down deep roots today. We need to develop deep roots while it is still day that when the night comes our faith will not be moved. The sun in the above parable represents the heat of trials that will test our faith. The reason the plant withered away was not as a result of the heat of the sun but rather was due to the lack of depth of the roots.

> *But he that received the seed into stony places, the same is he that hears the word, and soon with joy receiveth it; yet hath he not root in himself, but dureth for a while: for when tribulation or persecution arises because of the word, by and by he is offended (Matthew 13:20 -21).*

And *if thou faint in the day of adversity, thy strength is small (Proverbs 24:10).*

According to these two scriptures our strength is in our root structure. Proverbs 24 states: "if you faint your strength is small". Matthew 13 tells us that when adversity came they withered away because they had no root. In Matthew the hearer received the word, even with joy, when he was grafted into the True Vine, but he failed to invest the time to develop that root structure. Consequently he fainted and withered away in the day of adversity because his strength was small for he had no roots! We must develop this secret root structure with the Lord if we are to survive times of adversity.

How much of your spiritual life is hidden from view? How much time do you spend ministering to God alone in the Holy Place, compared to the time you spend ministering in the Outer Court before men? If all your spiritual life is exposed, then all your growth will be upwards like a weed, and because there is no downward growth, you lack deep roots! Roots are only cultivated in secret under the soil. Even when I am forcing spring bulbs in a glass container of water I must place the container in a dark closet until the roots begin to develop and to mature. Roots can only develop in the dark, in a secret place. Jesus instructs us how to develop our root structure in the book of Matthew: *but thou, when thou pray, enter into thy closet, (i.e. thine inner chamber, a hidden place) and when thou hast shut thy door, (shutting out the world and shutting yourself in with God) pray to thy Fa-*

ther which is in secret; and thy Father which seeth in secret shall reward thee openly (Matthew 6:6). If I live my whole spiritual life before men, and if I expose and show off my roots, I already have my reward that comes from the glory of man.

However if I live more of my life in secret in sweet communion with the Lord, He will reward me openly. If we expose our roots, they will wilt on the day of trials. Our roots are our source of survival on that day of trials, and if kept hidden, they will not wilt and fall away because of the heat. They are buried deep in the soil of our hearts, and are being fed hidden nourishment as we spend time alone with the Lord.

The root system of a plant is the most important part of the plant. Roots cannot be faked but fruit can sometimes be an imitation. For example, as a rose grower, I can detect when my roses have a sucker growing with the real thing. The sucker rose will be much smaller and lack depth of color and fragrance because it is not a product of the grafted root, but rather a product of a side shoot beneath the grafting. In fact, if the suckers are not cut off at the source, they will eventually zap the life of the plant. Spiritual gifts may be manifestation in the Outer Court of a spiritual root structure, BUT only intimacy with the Lord in the Holy of Holies can transform our character by developing deep roots in the True Vine, which we were crafted into when we were born again. The manifestation of the gifts is not a sign of a healthy spiritual root structure because they can be misused, abused or even faked. The Apostle Paul admonishes the believers in Corinth that although they came behind in no gift, they were carnal and still babes because they had not matured by displaying the fruit of the spirit. Only the fruit of the spirit is evidence of maturity of character. We cannot have the fruit without the root. That is the principle of sequence; private victory precedes public victory. In Genesis 32:24 Jacob was left alone. It was in this solitude that he had a defeat in the flesh and won a victory in the spirit. He had this private victory before a public victory, when He became the father of God's people, Israel. In other words the law of sowing and reaping, whatever you sow is hidden from view until it germinates to produce fruit that is manifested above the surface.

Thus, Jesus warns in Matthew: *wherefore by their fruits ye shall know them. Many will say to me in that day, Lord, Lord, have we not prophesied in thy name? And in thy name have cast out devils? And in thy name done many wonderful works? And then will I profess unto them, I never knew you: depart from me, ye that work iniquity (Matthew 7:20-23).* These obviously were manifested imitation giftings with no root structure in the True Vine.

The apostle Paul also warns us in his letter to the church at Corinth that *though I speak with the tongues of men and of angels, and have not charity, I am become as sounding brass, or a tinkling cymbal (1 Corinthians 13:1).* From this scripture, we are learning about the balance we must have between the fruit and the gifts of the spirit.

A fine type or picture of this truth is found in the Old Testament, from the hem of the priest's robe, where God commanded there be embroidered pomegranates and bells made of gold. They had to be arranged alternatively around the hem of the robe (read Exodus 39:24-25). If the bells were all placed together they would have clanged against each other and sounded like a cacophony instead of a symphony. The placement speaks to us of balance in our spiritual lives between the fruit and the gifts of the spirit. The pomegranates typify the fruit of the spirit. The golden bells speak of the gifts of the spirit. Surely if our lives do not minister the gifts through the fruit of the spirit, our lives would also make a clanging noise and be as sounding brass as Paul speaks of in 1 Corinthians 13:1.

So often are we out of balance, because we put too much emphasis on the gifts and neglect the fruit, which can only be matured as we spend time alone beholding Him where He will mold our character. This can only be achieved by developing a secret history with God and investing time in the root structure, so that the fruit of our lives may be the real thing, and bring glory to God and maturity to our walk with God, *that we might be called trees of righteousness, the planting of the Lord, that he might be glorified (Isaiah 61:3).* Matthew Henry states: "the Lord was to be the planter; for the church is God's husbandry, that they may be ornaments to God's vineyard and may be fruitful in the fruits of righteousness, as the branches of God's planting (Isaiah 60:21).

36

All that Christ does for us is to make us God's people, and some way serviceable to him as living trees, planted in the house of the Lord, and flourishing in the courts of our God; and all this that he may be glorified--that we bring forth much fruit."[7]

Our spiritual history begins the day the seed of the Word is planted in our hearts. Our growth to maturity depends on the watering and care of that seed that it might cultivate a healthy root structure producing the fruit of the spirit. God does not limit the progress of our growth, for He is limitless, we are the ones who limit our growth by not investing the time to develop a secret history with God.

He that dwelleth in the secret place of the most High shall abide under the shadow of the Almighty (Psalm 91:1).

---

[7] Matthew Henry, *Commentary*, Volume 4, MacDonald Publishing Company, 1985, p. 359.

CHAPTER TWO

INTIMACY THROUGH THE TABERNACLE

And there I will meet with thee, and I will commune with thee
from above the mercy seat, from between the two cherubims
which are upon the ark of the testimony (Exodus 25:22).

Because God acts in history, the flow of the Spirit is ever onwards. As we look at the layout of the Tabernacle (see the layout at the end of chapter) we catch a prophetic glimpse of God's dealing with His Church down through the ages. Even more importantly we see where God's spirit is moving today and why this will add dimension to our current study.

The blueprint of the Tabernacle was designed by God and given to Moses at the same time he received the Ten Commandments on Mount Sinai. It was the way God ordained for His people to approach His presence, a foreshadow of His plan of redemption, a prophetic tapestry woven in fine linens with accents of gold, silver and brass. The Tabernacle consisted of three sections. The Outer Court, which typifies the world and our ministry to the world. Within this Outer Court, God placed the Brazen Altar and the Brazen Laver. As we part the curtain separating the second section from the Outer Court, we enter the Holy Place, which typifies the church, the place of ministry to each other and fellowship of the saints. In the Holy Place we find the Golden Candlestick, the Golden Table of Shewbread and the Golden Altar of Incense. As we press on through the second veil, we approach the very presence of God, where His Shekinah glory dwelt above the Ark of the Covenant, in the Holy of Holies. I make reference to the Tabernacle so often in the message of this book because this layout was a map to show us the way into His Presence.

During the Middle Ages, also known as the dark ages, because the light of the true gospel was almost extinct, sinners tried to be saved by keeping the law, and paying for indulgences as a means of cleansing sin. But, thank God, even though the light was being snuffed out, God moved in the sixteenth century and raised up men like Martin Luther. who proclaimed Galatians 3:11: *but that no man is justified by the law in the sight of God, [it is] evident: for, The just shall live by faith.* These men restored to the Church the Brazen Altar, i.e. sinners can only be saved by faith in the Blood of Jesus. Brass in typology speaks of judgment. The Brazen Altar was a foreshadow of Christ, as the Lamb of God, being judged for the sins of the world. Out of the reformation that followed came the first translation of the Bible, preparing the way for the next move of God.

The Church remained in the Outer Court at the Brazen Altar, until the eighteenth century, when God raised up men like the

Wesley brothers who restored to the Church the Brazen Laver. Truly we are saved by the Blood, typified by the Brazen Altar. However, God wants not only a justified people but also a sanctified people who will press on in to serve Him in holiness. As the Brazen Altar spoke of Christ being judged for us, the Brazen Laver speaks of self-judgment. The Brazen Laver is a type of the Word of God, where we come daily to examine ourselves in the light of the Word, so that we may grow and mature.

At the turn of the twentieth century, we saw a mighty visitation of God throughout His Body, by an outpouring of His Holy Spirit, unprecedented in the history of the Church. The ministry of the Golden Candlestick had now been returned to the Church. The Golden Candlestick typifies the ministry and power of the Holy Spirit with the operations of the gifts within the Church. The restoration of the Candlestick has ignited the fire of Pentecost and is bringing unity to the Church, which will result in the oil to flow and power to fall.

Behold, how good and how pleasant [it is] for brethren to dwell together in unity! (Psalms 133:1).

It is like the precious ointment upon the head, that ran down upon the beard, [even] Aaron's beard: that went down to the skirts of his garments (Psalms 133:2).

As the Church moves ahead in one accord, we will see a great harvest of souls in these last days, for as Jesus prayed *that they all may be one; as thou, Father, [art] in me, and I in thee, that they also may be one in us: that the world may believe that thou hast sent me (John 17:21).*

This Pentecostal move of God, in turn led us to the restoration of the Golden Table of Shewbread, the place of fellowship. The only light in the Holy Place was the Golden Candlestick, by which the priests could see to have fellowship one with another at the Table of Shewbread. *But if we walk in the light, as he is in the light, we have fellowship one with another (1 John 1:7).* God has poured out His Holy Spirit upon all flesh and denominations. It wasn't until this time in history, that one could find believers from all denominations coming under one banner to glorify and lift up the name of Jesus, and have fellowship one with another as the Body and Bride of Christ. Our denominational badges could be looked upon as wrinkles in the wedding garment of His Bride, and through this move, God is ironing out those wrinkles, preparing His Bride for the marriage supper of the Lamb!

During the past few years, the flow of the Spirit has led the Church to the Golden Altar of Incense, teaching us to enter into true worship and praise, where once again the cloud of His Presence will cover us with His Glory. The ministry of the Golden Altar of Incense was not only the place of worship but also the place of prayer, where the priests would offer intercessory prayers on behalf of the people. I believe God is currently moving in this area as He is teaching His believer priests to pray, seek His Face, know and hear

His voice. He is restoring the Altar of Incense, the place of intimacy with Him, because the next and ultimate event on His timetable is when the Church steps beyond the torn veil into His Presence forever! *And I heard a great voice out of heaven saying, behold, the tabernacle of God [is] with men, and he will dwell with them, and they shall be his people, and God himself shall be with them, [and be] their God (Revelation 21:3).* His Church will be a bride washed in the blood of the Lamb at the Brazen Altar; a Bride matured through the Word at the Brazen Laver; a Bride moving in the power of the Holy Spirit at the Golden Candlestick; a Bride fellowshipping in unity at the Golden Table of Shewbread; a Bride investing time in an intimate relationship with Him offering praise that is acceptable in His Sight at the Golden Altar of Incense. Yes, all things will be restored on that day when according to Ephesians 5:27, *that he might present it to himself a glorious church, not having spot, or wrinkle, or any such thing; but that it should be holy and without blemish.*

However, until that day, if we want to be in the move of the Spirit, we must endeavor to invest time in our intimate relationship with the Lord, and restore the Golden Altar of Incense in our lives, for our bodies are the current temple of God. Since we are living in the 'last days' we need to have ears to hear what the Spirit is saying to the church of Laodicea, which is a prophetic analogy of the church in our day:

And unto the angel of the church of the Laodiceans write; These things saith the Amen, the faithful and true witness, the beginning of the creation of God; I know thy works, that thou art neither cold nor hot: I would thou wert cold or hot. So then because thou art lukewarm, and neither cold nor hot, I will spue thee out of my mouth. Because thou sayest, I am rich, and increased with goods, and have need of nothing; and knowest not that thou art wretched, and miserable, and poor, and blind, and naked: I counsel thee to buy of me gold tried in the fire, that thou mayest be rich; and white raiment, that thou mayest be clothed, and that the shame of thy nakedness do not appear; and anoint thine eyes with eyesalve, that thou mayest see. As many as I love, I rebuke and chasten: be zealous therefore, and repent. Behold, I stand at the door, and knock: if any man hear my voice, and open the door, I will come in to him, and will sup with him, and he with me (Revelation 3:14-20).

Remember this word is not written to the world, it is a warning to the church. Much of the church today has fallen into apathy, neither cold nor hot. The state of our nation and even some of those within the church held to the opinion, that while the economy was good, it didn't matter about morality. Our moral fiber is unraveling while we are being deceived by the possibility of a good economy again and riches. Read again how Jesus admonishes this church: *you say, 'I am rich; I have acquired wealth and do not need a thing.' But you do not realize that you are wretched, pitiful, poor, blind and naked (Revelation 3:17).* Yes, even when we may have a good economy, we are still morally bankrupt. What will we, the church, do about this? Bear in mind that we are the salt and light of the world. Will we take a stand, even if it touches our pocket book and could mean persecution if we do not bow to the throne of political correctness? We will probably only be prepared to take a stand for righteousness if we have developed deep spiritual roots, otherwise the heat of persecution will cause our shallow faith to wilt.

I believe that the shallow roots and apathy are a direct result of lack of intimacy with the Lord. The Laodicea church was the church that shut Him out. They enjoyed their 'self- made' riches while forgetting the source of their blessings. If we want to be overcomers in these last days, we must restore the Golden Altar of Incense in our lives, by spending time alone with God, so that He might nourish and strengthen our root structure. Only this will result in a character of integrity and conviction that will be able to stand the test of the heat of trials and persecution.

The church on earth today has inherited vast wealth from those who have gone before us. We cannot overestimate the greatness of our spiritual heritage, nor be sufficiently grateful to God for it. But if today you try to be a 'Luther' or a 'Wesley', you will miss your destiny or why you have come to the Kingdom for such a time as this. You will fall short of the purpose of God for this generation, for you will be moving backwards while the tide of the Spirit is flowing onwards.

Who knoweth whether thou art come to the kingdom for such a time as this? (Esther 4:14).

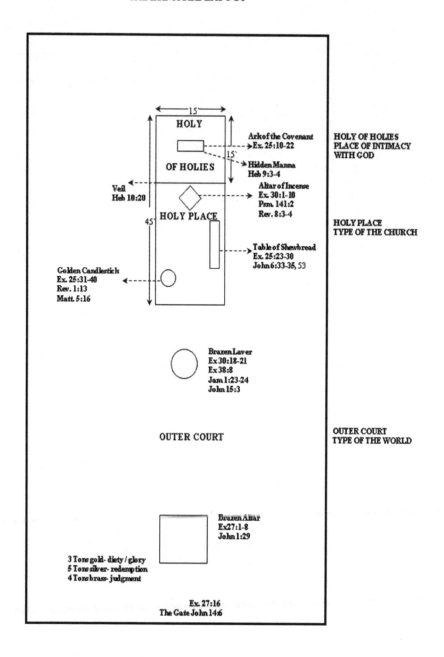

HOLY

OF HOLIES

HOLY PLACE

OUTER COURT

15

15'

45'

Veil
Heb 10:20

Golden Candlestick
Ex. 25:31-40
Rev. 1:13
Matt. 5:16

Ark of the Covenant
Ex. 25:10-22

Hidden Manna
Heb 9:3-4

Altar of Incense
Ex. 30:1-10
Psm. 141:2
Rev. 8:3-4

Table of Shewbread
Ex. 25:23-30
John 6:33-35, 53

Brazen Laver
Ex 30:18-21
Ex 38:8
Jam 1:23-24
John 15:3

Brazen Altar
Ex 27:1-8
John 1:29

3 Tons gold- diety / glory
5 Tons silver- redemption
4 Tons brass- judgment

Ex. 27:16
The Gate John 14:6

HOLY OF HOLIES
PLACE OF INTIMACY
WITH GOD

HOLY PLACE
TYPE OF THE CHURCH

OUTER COURT
TYPE OF THE WORLD

CHAPTER THREE
WHY DO WE STRUGGLE?

For the flesh lusteth against the Spirit, and the Spirit against the flesh: and these are contrary the one to the other: so that ye cannot do the things that ye would (Galatians 5:17).

I think we would all agree that this one area, of faithfully spending time alone with God, is the area we struggle with as believers more than any other aspect of our Christian walk. In all other aspects of our walk we have others who can hold us accountable, but this is one area where we have to hold ourselves accountable. This is the part of our spiritual history that is hidden from the view of others, known only to the Lord and ourselves. The enemy is always at hand to offer justifiable excuses to muffle our conscience, because he knows the spiritual power in the life of a believer who spends time in the Father's presence. We are engaged in spiritual warfare as we endeavor to set aside this precious time to press on in. Having been there many times myself I cried out in desperation: "teach me, Lord, to draw near that I may truly worship you! Why do I struggle with drawing near to be alone with You, when I know it is a privilege, and that privilege had an awesome price?"

Is this the cry of your heart? Let us look at some of the excuses we may find hidden in the recesses of our hearts. Which of the following would be your excuse?

1. So busy that you don't have the time?
2. Cannot be bothered?
3. Left your first love?
4. Unbelief?
5. Guilt?
6. Fear of spiritual warfare and discouragement?
7. Too tired and weary or lazy?

I believe I have heard them all during my years of ministry, and I have been there at them all sometime during my Christian walk. Truly the spirit is willing but the flesh is so weak!

Our longings for God cause us to be spiritually hungry. Because the pangs of hunger hurt, we try to take the edge off the hunger any way we can. One of those ways is religious activity of reading books, listening to tapes or going to seminars. Through these avenues, which are often good, even nourishing, we are still only being fed second hand manna because they are the experiences of others. God wants to feed each of us personally, hidden manna, as we dedicate the time to fellowship alone with Him in the Holy of Holies. So often our 'busyness' is in the Outer Court, where we feel we are redeeming our time and making the best use of our time, and all the while God is beckoning us to press on in through the torn veil and draw near to Him in the Holy of Holies.

> *Dear Child,*
> *Your time spent with me is the greatest investment in life. If you don't spend time with Me you will have nothing to give others that has life in it; for only life begets life. Don't waste your days sowing seeds of the flesh, because flesh can never beget spirit. Every seed begets after its own kind. That is the law of the universe. You can only receive spiritual seeds of me. If you love Me you will want to spend time with Me, not only to receive spiritual seeds from Me, but to just be with Me.*
> *Thus saith Papa.*

Behold, I stand at the door, and knock: if any man hear my voice, and open the door, I will come in to him, and will sup with him, and he with me (Revelation 3:20).

Will the excuses that rob us of our precious time with Papa really matter in the light of eternity?

Excuse 1 - So busy that you don't have the time.

Of all the excuses I have heard over years of ministry, and the excuse I've used most often myself, this has to be the number one reason we do not spend quality time with our Heavenly Father. In the high pace world we live in, time is a rare commodity. We are too busy to spend time with friends, family and even too busy to invest time alone with God. This results in relationships with shallow roots because no investment has been made.

49

What is life all about? It is all about relationships: first with God, and then with others. Time once spent is gone forever, so invest it wisely. We may wake up one morning and find we are living with a stranger as a spouse, and our children are grown up and gone, leaving only regret that we didn't spend more time with them. We have no true friends, and although we have been introduced to our Heavenly Father, we lack confidence in our relationship to Him, and do not recognize His voice. When God drew up the blueprint for our life and destiny, He allotted time for us to spend with Him. So if we are too busy, we are either trying to achieve more than He requires of us, or we are involved in matters outside His will for us. We need to understand that it is not a matter of time, but rather it is a matter of choice. Jesus said Mary had "chosen the good part". If we are short of time, the better choice would be to do less FOR God, that we may have time to be WITH God. Martha was so busy doing for Jesus. Mary chose to do less in order to spend time with Jesus.

We are all given twenty-four hours in a day, how will you spend them? Your choices are your priorities. The Word tells us "for where your treasure is, there will your heart be also". Time is a treasure. In a hunger to invest my time to know my heavenly Papa more intimately I cried this prayer:

Help me daily to see you in the windows of my soul that you provide, that I might know you more and more. And with Your help and strength, Papa, may I daily be conformed to Your image. Papa, I am seeking to know You, not just an introduction to You and fellowship with Your family. But, Papa, I am seeking quality and intimate time with You alone, that you may burn off the dross and replace it as you form and mold me to Your likeness, deep down in my innermost being, in my root structure that I may bear the fruit of the spirit and not the flesh.

Papa answered my cry with this admonishment:

Dear Child,
That is why it is so important to abide in Me. Only then can I daily work on your heart to conform you. As I am conforming you, you learn and understand My heart more, and our relationship is deepened, and your root structure becomes deep and strong in Me. Then your life will bear much fruit as you work with the Spirit in the fields I send you to! Child, hold unto these times with Me, they are precious, and the enemy will do anything to steal them from you! Daily learn of Me and daily learn from Me.
Thus saith Papa.

All too often we take time to be introduced to our Heavenly Father but fail to take the time needed to develop that relationship with Him. I have always struggled with trying to make my day productive. I thought I was obeying the command to *"redeeming the time, because the days are evil" (Ephesians 5:16).*

My Heavenly Papa changed my thinking with this word:

51

Dear Child,

Redeeming the time is not being busy, busy, busy! But rather it is investing your life in that which I have called you to do.

You are redeeming the time as you talk with Me and listen to My voice. You are redeeming the time while you are resting in Me. While resting in Me you commune with Me; While you commune with Me I will refresh you.

As I refresh you I will renew your strength, to do that which I want you to do.

Burnout comes from doing more than I ask or give the grace for you to do. If I haven't required it of you, the grace is not present, if the grace is not present, you will have to work in the flesh, which will cause sweat and burn you out.

Come and learn of Me, my yoke is light! Don't burn your energy out on the lesser; conserve it for the greater.

Passion ignites fire to create energy, don't squander it on a lesser passion. Don't give your greatest passion the leftovers. I know all your needs and responsibilities of everyday life, but seek first My Kingdom and all these things will be added unto you. A full life is not a life of "busyness" but rather a full life is a life full of Me!

Thus saith Papa.

I have grown to hate the phrase 'too busy', and yet I realize that God wants His children to be responsible and accountable in all areas of their lives. Feeling confused I asked the Lord:

When is being busy only busyness, and when is being busy, responsible and accountable?

I received the following answer:

Dear Child,
It is busyness when it keeps you from time of reflection and
time alone with Me.
It is the motivation that is the answer. If you are too busy to
spend time with Me, you are guilty of the sin of presump-
tion, because you are doing more than I'm asking of you.
When I planned your life, I planned for you to have time to
fellowship with Me.
If you are too busy to spend time with Me, you are honoring
other things in your life before Me and above Me.
If your busyness is to avoid time with Me, it is a cover up
and you are not being true to yourself. Being responsible and
accountable is being a faithful servant of what I have placed
before you and using your talents and giftings wisely and
redeeming your time as I direct you.
Thus saith Papa.

Recently I was sent the following over the internet, and although the author is unknown, it is so applicable to this area of busyness; I had to interject it here:

Satan called a worldwide convention. In his opening address to his Evil demons, he said: "We cannot keep the Christians from going to church. We cannot keep them from reading their Bibles and knowing the truth! We cannot even keep them from forming an intimate, abiding relationship experience in Christ. If they gain that connection with Jesus, our power over them is broken. So let them go to their churches, let them have their conservative lifestyles, but steal their time, so they cannot gain that experience in Jesus Christ. This is what I want you to do demons. Distract them from gaining hold of their Savior and maintaining that vital connection throughout their day! "How shall we do this?" shouted his demons.

"Keep them busy in the nonessentials of life and invent innumerable schemes to occupy their minds," he answered. Tempt them to spend, spend, spend, and borrow, borrow, borrow.

Persuade the wives to go to work for long hours and the husbands to work 6-7 days a week, 10-12 hours a day, so they can afford their empty lifestyles. Keep them from spending time with their children. As their family fragments, soon their home will offer no escape from the pressures of work! Over-stimulate their minds so that they cannot hear that still, small voice. Entice them to play the radio or cassette player whenever they drive. To keep the TV, VCR CDs and their PCs going constantly in their homes. And see to it that every store and restaurant in the world plays non-biblical music constantly. This will jam their minds and break that union with Christ. Fill the coffee table with magazines and newspapers.

Pound their minds with the news 24 hours a day. Invade their driving moments with billboards. Flood their mailboxes with junk mail, mail order catalogues, sweepstakes, and every kind of news-letter and promotional offering free products, services, and false hopes. Keep skinny, beautiful models on the magazines so the husbands will believe that external beauty is what's important, and they'll become dissatisfied with their wives.

Ha! That will fragment those families quickly! Even in their recrea-tion, let them be excessive. Have them return from their recreation exhausted, disquieted, and unprepared for the coming week.

Don't let them go out in nature to reflect on God's wonders. Send them to amusement parks, sporting events, concerts and movies instead. Keep them busy, busy, busy!!! And when they meet for spiritual fellowship, involve them in gossip and small talk so that they leave with troubled consciences and unsettled emotion. Go ahead, let them be involved in soul winning. But crowd their lives with so many good causes they have no time to seek power from Christ. Soon they will be working in their own strength, sacrificing their health and family for the good of the cause. It will work! It will work!

It was quite a convention. And the evil demons went eagerly to their assignments causing Christians everywhere to get busy, busy, busy and to rush here and there.

I guess the question is: has the devil been successful at his scheme? You be the judge! When the children of Israel commenced to plan their exodus from Egypt, to spend time with God in the wilderness, the reaction of Pharaoh was to double their labor so that they had no time even to think about it (see Exodus 5:1-13). When you begin to plan or practice a more effective prayer life, Satan will counter by making you busier than ever with needs and responsibilities, so that you have no time for prayer.

You must not neglect your duties nor fail to take your responsibilities seriously, but you should put prayer first. In this realm the principle of tithing may also be helpful. After you have given God a tenth, you will discover that you can more efficiently use the remaining nine-tenths of your time, instead of being:

> ➢ B - Being
> ➢ U - Under
> ➢ S - Satan's
> ➢ Y - Yoke

Are you too BUSY?

Excuse 2 – Just cannot be bothered

Behind this excuse is a heart that has grown lukewarm due to prideful roots that has caused us to arrogantly feel we can survive spiritually without this time with the Father. Consequently we could be compared to the church of Laodicea who had grown lukewarm and thought they were so self-sufficient they had need of nothing, or like Israel in the time of Jeremiah: *O generation, see ye the word of the Lord. Have I been a wilderness unto Israel? A land of darkness? Wherefore say my people, we are lords; we will come no more unto thee? (Jeremiah 2:31).*

But the lack of desire cannot be blamed on the lukewarmness of the heart, because it is only a consequence of something more serious, yet more dangerous because it is so subtle, it is the consequence of self-sufficiency. That life of self-sufficiency shuts out the warmth and light of His Face, causing our hearts to grow cold. When Jesus died, the veil outside the Holy of Holies was rent from top to bottom, to avail us once again of the warmth of His presence. But our self-sufficiency is like a veil over our hearts shutting out the warmth of that presence. The sins of the self-life are so subtle because they are not something we DO but rather they are something we ARE!

From these prideful roots of self-sufficiency sprouts other self-life sins such as self-righteousness, self-pity, self-confidence, self-admiration, and a host of others like them. How do we rent or remove this opaque veil of self-sufficiency from our hearts, that the warmth of His presence may melt our cold indifference and apathy? We cannot rent the veil ourselves. A.W. Tozer warns us in his book *The Pursuit of God* that "we dare not tinker with our inner life, hoping to rend the veil ourselves. God must do it for us. Our part is to yield and trust. We must confess and forsake the self-life and then reckon it crucified. We dare not rest content with a neat doctrine of self-crucifixion."[8]

Are prideful self-sufficient hearts going to prevent us from partaking in the feast that He has prepared for us during our time of fellowship with Him?

Again, he sent forth other servants, saying, Tell them which are bidden, Behold, I have prepared my dinner: my oxen and my fatlings are killed, and all things are ready: come unto the marriage. But they made light of it, and went their ways, one to his farm, another to his merchandise (Matthew 22:4-5).

Matthew Henry's Commentary states:

The reason they made light of it was because they had other things that their minds were more on. The business and profit of worldly employment prove to many a great hindrance in closing with Christ. It is true that both farmers and merchants must be diligent in their business but not so to keep them from making religion their main business. *Licitis perimus omnes* - These lawful things undo us - when they are unlawfully managed, when we are so careful and troubled about many things as to neglect the one thing needful.[9]

In yielding we are humbling ourselves before Him, demonstrating that we are not self-sufficient: *not that we are sufficient of ourselves to think anything as of ourselves; but our sufficiency is of God (2 Corinthians 3:5);* while confirming our need that *man shall not live by bread alone, but by every word that proceedeth out of the mouth of God (Matthew 4:4).* Only an earnest craving for that hidden manna will ignite a fire of passionate desire to spend time with our heavenly Papa. It is not

[8] A. W. Tozer, "The Pursuit of God," Christian Publications, 1982, p. 30.
[9] Matthew Henry, *Commentary,* Volume 5, MacDonald Publishing Company, 1985, p. 313.

the apathetic prayer which availeth much but rather, the Word tells us, it is *the effectual fervent prayer of a righteous man availeth much (James 5:16)*.

We cannot seek Him half heartily but rather we must seek Him with all our hearts.

Excuse 3 – Left your first love

> *I know thy works, and thy labour, and thy patience, and how thou canst not bear them which are evil: and thou hast tried them which say they are apostles, and are not, and hast found them liars: And hast borne, and hast patience, and for my name's sake hast laboured, and hast not fainted. Nevertheless I have somewhat against thee, because thou hast left thy first love (Revelation 2:2-4).*

God was aware of all their labors for Him and yet He still had something against them - they had left their First Love. Our redemption bought back that which was lost in the garden. What did we lose in the Garden? We lost our fellowship with God! Are we hiding in the Outer Court covering our nakedness with the leaves of good works when God is calling to us "where are you?" Is our response "God I don't have time to spend with you today BUT I am doing all this for You?" Watchman Nee writes: "there we cannot pretend or hide our condition. Pretense is not Christianity; it is only a covering for our wretchedness. Pretense is opposite of INTEGRITY because it is deceit, double dealing and faithlessness. While we are trying to cover something we are not naked or totally honest with God. He starts with a Jacob and ends with an Israel."[10] And all the while God is beckoning:

Child,
Spend time with Me in the Holy of Holies and I will give
you a covering of white raiment.
Thus saith Papa.

Once again, God is more interested in what we are becoming than what we are doing. And we only become like Him as we spend time with Him and behold Him. Truly we become what we see or hear. Consider the influences your peers have had in your life, good or bad, they made an impact. May we all be *looking unto Jesus the author and finisher of our faith! (Hebrews 12:2).*

Have we been so busy in the Outer Court ministering to men and doing work for His Kingdom that we have forgotten to minister to the King? Have we been so busy studying the Word that we have forgotten the Author? Reading and learning the scriptures must do more than cause us to be Bible literate, it must lead us to know the Father! This was the cry of my heart as I prayed the following:

Open my eyes this day to see YOU in the scriptures. How
can I see except by the Holy Spirit? Save and protect me, I
pray, from reasoning and personal interpretation of your
Word. May I totally rely on the urging and teaching of the

---

[10] Watchman Nee, *The Joyful Heart Daily Meditations*, Devotion March 21, Tyndale House Publishers, 1978.

Holy Spirit! May I know by the burning in my heart, that it is Your unveiling of the scriptures.

And the answer I received was:

Dear Child,
If it is alive and brings life, it is My teaching!
If it reveals and unveils ME, it is alive, for I am the living Word.
The reasoning of the mind can only teach the cold letter of the Word. My teaching has the spiritual dimension of life and has anointing and power. The intellectual teaching of the Word can change minds BUT will never change hearts. To change hearts and give life it must have the anointing of spiritual life!
It is more than an exchange of words, it is breathing life.
Thus saith Papa.

Who also hath made us able ministers of the New Testament; not of the letter, but of the spirit: for the letter killeth but the spirit giveth life (2 Corinthians 3:6).

Even some who call themselves theologians can know the Scriptures, yet may not know the Author. Many may quote the twenty-third Psalm without knowing the Shepherd. Yes, of course, we need to read and even memorize the scriptures, but not at the neglect of truly seeking to know the heart of the Father.

For when religion has its last word, there is little that we need other than God Himself. The ancient Westminster catechism reads,

"What is the chief end of man? Man's chief end is to glorify God and enjoy Him forever."[11]

> *Dear Child,*
>
> *Many invite Me into their lives and then ignore Me! And don't have time for Me! How quickly they have left their first love!*
>
> *Which of you would invite, even compel a guest to come and live with you, and then you ignore that guest, you don't even talk with that guest?*
>
> *Which of you do not do all you can to make a guest feel at home and comfortable? Yet many quench and grieve My spirit by what they do, what they say and by what they have in their home! They don't even clean their home when I come to abide with them. They shut off certain rooms to My presence, lest I cleanse these areas.*
>
> *Am I a welcomed guest, or am I only a tolerated guest to ease your conscience?*
>
> *You will not have peace while ignoring or striving against Me!*
>
> *Do I have the seat of the honored guest, the Lord of all? Or am I only the Savior you have forgotten?*
>
> *Am I crowned Lord of all in your life?*
>
> *Yielding to My Spirit and surrendering to the Spirit is crowning Me 'The Lord of All'.*
>
> *Thus saith Papa.*

---

[11]Thomas Vincent, *Westminster Shorter Catechism*, 1675.

Excuse 4 – Unbelief

Do we really believe that through our quiet prayer time we can indeed converse with the King of kings, who is our Heavenly Father? I have often asked myself that question, and realized that if I believed that with all my heart, I would not have a struggle to set apart that time. How many of us would not have the time, if given the opportunity, of a private audience with The Queen of England or the President of the USA? The One who is offering us a private audience is the Lord of lords and Everlasting Father! Do we believe it or have we taken His invitation for granted?

> But without faith it is impossible to please him: for he that cometh to God must believe that he is, and that he is a rewarder of them that diligently seek him (Hebrew11:6).

> I will therefore that men pray everywhere, lifting up holy hands, without wrath and doubting (1 Timothy 2:8).

When we are lacking faith we need to give it a dose of the Word: *So then faith cometh by hearing, and hearing by the word of God (Romans 10:17).* Meditate upon, chew over and feed your faith on the following Scriptures:

> Call unto me, and I will answer thee, and show thee great and mighty things, which thou knowest not (Jeremiah 33:3).

> And it shall come to pass, that before they call, I will answer; and while they are yet speaking, I will hear (Isaiah 65:24).

> To him the porter openeth; and the sheep hear his voice: and he calleth his own sheep by name, and leadeth them out (John 10:3).

My sheep hear my voice, and I know them, and they follow me (John10:27).

We know that the heathen serve gods that cannot hear, speak or see: *the idols of the heathen are silver and gold, the work of men's hands. They have mouths, but they speak not; eyes have they, but they see not; They have ears, but they hear not; neither is there any breath in their mouths (Psalm 135:15-17).* Dare we doubt that our Almighty God, who made our ears and mouths, does not hear nor speak? *Yet they say, The Lord shall not see, neither shall the God of Jacob regard it. Understand, ye brutish among the people: and ye fools, when will ye be wise? He that planted the ear, shall he not hear? He that formed the eye, shall he not see? (Psalm 94:7-9).* (See chapter on "How do I Hear His voice?").

Excuse 5 – Guilt

And there I will meet with thee, and I will commune with thee from above the mercy seat, from between the two cherubims which are upon the ark of the testimony (Exodus 25:22).

In Ancient Israel, the High Priest had to go alone into the Holy of Holies to minister unto God. We enter the Holy of Holies of our temple by searching our innermost being. We, like the High Priest, must also go alone, and there God will meet with us.

That is why so many are reluctant to enter in and draw near. For as we search our hearts we see ourselves as we really are. Only when we are prepared to spend the time and have the courage to truly look inside ourselves and examine the authenticity of our lives, are we being totally honest and naked before God. This is true intimacy and the place where our secret history with God will grow. Since our inner most being is the present Holy of Holies where God dwells in us, it is the place of our authentic inner life, and nobody knows the condition of that life except God. Without the blood we would not have the courage to see ourselves as we really are. Without the cleansing blood we would not have the boldness to enter and be alone with God.

We will often want to avoid being totally honest with ourselves because in His Presence is only TRUTH and that which is not truth, He will consume that we may be blameless before Him. Frequently we will offer Him only lip service in the Outer Court due to a lack of confidence in our relationship with Him, because we know of attitudes, habits, or sin in our lives, which He, as a loving Father, would reveal if we pressed on into His presence. So rather than face Him, we busy ourselves in the Outer Court ministering for Him when we should be in Holy of Holies ministering unto Him.

The enemy has us chained to the Outer Court by 'little foxes' to avoid us entering into the anointing and power of His presence. Once again the 'good', because the outer court ministry is good, robs us of the 'best'. We become so busy, stressed and burned out because much of what we are trying to accomplish is by the sweat of our brow and not by His Spirit.

May we all with sincerity of heart pray: "Oh! Lord, restore in my life the Golden Altar of Incense that I may be ready to meet You face to face!"

Dear Child,
Many avoid my presence because they don't want to spend time in My Word and be cleansed at the Laver*. Then they don't have the confidence needed to draw near the Golden Candlestick** which would reveal their sin and their avoidance of being cleansed at the Laver by applying the water of the Word.
Thus saith Papa.

Beloved, if our heart condemn us not, then have we confidence toward God (1 John 3:21).

*The Laver was a brass bowl lined in mirrors and filled with water. It was placed outside the Holy Place, where the priests would look inside it and cleanse themselves, before entering into the Holy Place, "lest they die," says the Word in Exodus 30:21. It is a type of the Word of God, since it was brass which speaks of self-judgment, and filled with water, reminding us of the cleansing power of the Word. Do we avoid the Brazen Laver because we do not want to pray?

"Search me, O God, and know my heart: try me, and know my thoughts: And see if there be any wicked way in me, and lead me in the way everlasting" (Psalm 137:23-24).

**The Golden Candlestick, which lit up the Holy Place, speaks of the ministry of the Holy Spirit, as He searches, empowers and matures the church.

What 'little foxes' has the enemy used to keep you chained to the Outer Court and caused you to lack confidence to enter in and draw near to Papa?

Is the lack of confidence that is causing you to shy from His presence, due to a guilty conscience, or due to condemnation that the enemy has sown in your mind? While personally asking myself the same question, the Lord gave me this word of encouragement:

> *Dear Child,*
>
> *If you adhere to my chastisement through conviction there will be no avenue or foothold for the enemy to drown you in condemnation and rob you of the joy of your salvation. Do not give place to him, for he goes about as a roaring lion seeking whom he may devour and destroy.*
>
> *Conviction is the voice of the conscience by the Holy Spirit.*
> *Condemnation is self-destructive thoughts of the mind from the enemy.*
> *Conviction is a warning that provides a choice and healing.*
> *Condemnation offers only hopelessness with no healing but rather incurableness.*
> *There is hope in Christ Jesus!*
> *There is healing in Christ Jesus!*
> *There is forgiveness in Christ Jesus!*
> *There is mercy in Christ Jesus!*

He came into the world NOT to condemn it but to save it. I send conviction because I love you! The enemy sows condemnation because he wants to destroy you!
Conviction will mature you!
Condemnation will destroy you!
Thus saith Papa.

The Websters dictionary defines 'conviction' as "the state of being convinced of error or compelled to admit the truth," and the Oxford dictionary defines condemnation as "being pronounced forfeited or unfit for use or incurable; being pronounced guilty." The Holy Spirit convicts our hearts to warn us of sin in our lives. The conviction gives us a chance to respond and be cleansed and healed. Whereas the enemy, through condemnation, tries to rob us of the forgiveness that was paid for by the Blood of Jesus. Remember that Satan is the accuser of the brethren, but we have an advocate with the Father, who ever lives to make intercession for us.

If the answer is a guilty conscience, run to Him not from Him. Therapists may be able to help you deal with your past but cannot help you with the black mark of guilt on your conscience. There is only One who has the power to cleanse the slate, the One who promises *"I, even I, am he that blotteth out thy transgressions for mine own sake, and will not remember thy sins" (Isaiah 43: 25).* If there is an outstanding offense on your conscience, confess it to God, that the enemy may not have a hold over you.

As the Lord Jesus tells his disciples in the Garden of Gethsemane, *hereafter I will not talk much with you: for the prince of this world cometh, and hath nothing in me (John 14:30).* Obviously, as the sinless Son of God, the enemy had nothing to hold over Him as He had a clear conscience before God and man. Likewise if we clear our conscience before God as the Word tells us: *if we confess our sins, he is faithful and just to forgive us our sins, and to cleanse us from all unrighteousness (John 1:9);* we should also clear our conscience before men, *therefore if thou bring thy gift to the altar, and there rememberest that thy brother hath ought against thee; Leave there thy gift before the altar, and go thy way; first be reconciled to thy brother, and then come and offer thy gift (Matthew 5:23-24).* Then the enemy will have nothing to hold over us. We will also be following Paul's footsteps who declares: *and herein do I exercise myself, to have always a conscience void of offence toward God, and toward men (Acts 24:16).* Then the enemy will not be able to rob us of our confidence to draw near to God.

If the answer is condemnation, you should claim this verse: *there is therefore now no condemnation to them which are in Christ Jesus, who walk not after the flesh, but after the Spirit (Romans 8:1).* And remember: *for God sent not his Son into the world to condemn the world; but that the world through him might be saved (John 3:17).* If your conscience is clear before God, do not let the enemy steal the joy of your salvation, which is restored fellowship with your Heavenly Father.

Adam hid from His presence because of the guilt of sin. However, we do not have that excuse because of the provision He has made for us through the cleansing Blood. Once again we have the privilege of fellowship with Him.

Excuse 6 – Fear of spiritual warfare

While we are pressing on into His presence to commune with Him, we have moved to the frontline of spiritual warfare and will become a target of the enemy. Will we retreat in defeat or will we stay engaged by praying through to victory? Standing our ground by claiming: *ye are of God, little children, and have overcome them: because greater is he that is in you, than he that is in the world (1 John 4:4).* Fear can take you to the place where your courage is stored.

I am reminded of a story when my girls were very young. We had been traveling all weekend in ministry and arrived home at four in the early morning, physically and spiritually exhausted, to find the windows on the car that we had left behind, vandalized and smashed. Our youngest daughter, Kathleen, who was then only ten, responded with, "we must have made the devil mad this weekend." Talk about, out of the mouths of babies. To explain this better, the girls had been going through a time of persecution and ridicule at school by their peers who lived close by, after they discovered the girls were gospel recording artists. We never found out who vandalized the car but assumed it was those peers who had been leaving us horrible and frightening messages on our answering machine every weekend. Our daughters had learned at a very tender age to stand their ground, by being aware that they have to *be sober, be vigilant; because your adversary the devil, as a roaring lion, walketh about, seeking whom he may devour (1 Peter 5:8).* We had read the book *Pilgrims Progress* with the girls for years, and from this they had understood that the roaring lion had no teeth!

As born again believers we are all enrolled in the army of the Lord. Timothy, in his epistles, exhorts us to be good soldiers. Soldiers are trained for battle and to engage the enemy. We are expected not only to withhold our ground against the enemy, but also to gain ground for the Kingdom. Ephesians chapter 6:10-18 provides our armor for the battle. The most neglected exhortation on the armor is verse 18: *"praying always with all prayer and supplication in the Spirit, and watching thereunto with all perseverance and supplication for all saints" (Ephesians 6:18).* Praying in the Spirit is the oil that prevents the rest of the armor from becoming rusty. The greatest spiritual battles we will ever fight are those fought on our knees!

In Daniel 10:12-13, the curtains are pulled back that we might see into this spiritual warfare, where Daniel's answer to prayer is delayed three weeks, due to war in the heavenlies between holy angels and unholy angels. We are given another glimpse of this conflict here: *"and there was war in heaven: Michael and his angels fought against*

70

the dragon; and the dragon fought and his angels" (Revelation 12:7). We may still be waiting for an answer, but we must stay in the battle, keep praying, because our "Michael", our Great High Priest, is ever making intercession for us. We are withdrawing from the battle if we stop praying; and we are surrendering if we cease pressing through. Take encouragement from Peter's conversation with the Lord: *"and the Lord said, Simon, Simon, behold, Satan hath desired to have you, that he may sift you as wheat: But I have prayed for thee, that thy faith fail not: and when thou art converted, strengthen thy brethren" (Luke 22:31-32).*

Are we soldiers who are "Absent Without Leave" due to a lack of courage to engage the enemy on our knees? Do we have a choice if we are to survive in the Lord's army? Be of good courage and meditate upon this scripture: *"wait on the Lord: be of good courage, and he shall strengthen thine heart: wait, I say, on the Lord" (Psalm 27:14).*

Spiritual battles or circumstances in our lives will either cause us to grow or to backslide, depending on our response. Remember it is the same sun that causes wax to melt or clay to harden; it is the same heat of trials that will cause our hearts to soften or harden. They will cause us to grow, if we exercise our spiritual muscles and stay in the battle, or they will cause us to backslide, if we surrender to the enemy and give up. Don't be discouraged by circumstances. God often allows circumstances that we may lay aside daily living just to see what is behind the circumstances. In other words He often uses these circumstances to get our attention, so we will draw near to Him. God used a burning bush to get Moses' attention. However, it wasn't until the Lord saw that Moses turned to see, did the Lord call to him.

And when the Lord saw that he turned aside to see, God called unto him out of the midst of the bush, and said, Moses, Moses. And he said, Here am I (Exodus 3: 4).

When we "turn aside to see" we will hear His voice calling to us out of the circumstance. How repeatedly have we been brought to our knees in fervent prayer because of an adverse situation in our lives?

Excuse 7 – Too tired and weary or lazy

And let us not be weary in well doing: for in due season we shall reap, if we faint not (Galatians 6:9).

As disciples of the Lord Jesus, we are to follow in His footsteps, who though weary, still pressed on to do the will of His Father. We read in the Bible that: *now Jacob's well was there. Jesus therefore, being wearied with his journey sat thus on the well: and it was about the sixth hour (John 4: 6).* We find Him still doing the Father's will. He was weary, He was hungry, yet when His disciples returned with food, He amazed them by saying: *but he said unto them, I have meat to eat that ye know not of. Therefore said the disciples one to another, Hath any man brought him ought to eat? Jesus saith unto them, My meat is to do the will of him that sent me, and to finish his work (John 4:32-34).* Here we see Jesus weary and yet, He still ministers to the woman at the well. How often are we weary on our pilgrim journey? And yet rather than pressing on we just give up and console ourselves with the idea that there is always tomorrow. If only we could see that pressing on to do His will, even when we are tired, would refresh us and give us strength, i.e. meat that we don't know or understand. That supernatural strength comes in doing His will. Remember the Scripture that says: *but they that wait upon the Lord shall renew their strength; they shall mount up with wings as eagles; they shall run, and not be weary; and they shall walk, and not faint (Isaiah 40:31).* As we wait upon the Lord, that is to serve Him as we minister unto Him, our strength shall be renewed.

> *Who among you would say to your slave who has just come in from plowing or tending sheep in the field, 'Come here at once and take your place at the table'? Would you not rather say to him, 'Prepare supper for me, put on your apron and serve me while I eat and drink; later you may eat and drink'? Do you thank the slave for doing what was commanded? So you also, when you have done all that you were ordered to do, say, 'We are worthless slaves; we have done only what we ought to have done!' (Luke 17:7-10).*

We may often feel weary from working in the fields that He has sent us to, but that is no excuse to neglect to serve and minister unto Him. This is where my heart was when I prayed this prayer:

> *Father,*
> *Forgive me for the times I grow so weary working for You, that I become a lazy and unworthy servant, because I don't wait on You and serve You. Forgive me for feeling I have done my duty by being busy in the Outer Court, and I neglect to draw near and serve You, by offering You my praise and glorifying Your name! And having served You with the fruit of my lips, staying at Your feet that You may feed me*

that hidden manna that satisfies my soul and feeds my
spirit! May I sup with You!

The Lord chastised me with the following words;

Dear Child,
What you do, is a duty! What you are becoming in My
presence is a relationship, based on love, trust, and reverent
fear. Invest in the relationship and the duty will not be a
burden, but rather an extension of the relationship, as I work
through you in the world.
Learn of Me for I am meek and lowly in heart and you will
find rest, even while you are working.
Thus saith Papa.

Surely we must go the second mile!

Matthew Henry's commentary: "whatever we do for Christ, we must be very humble, and not imagine we can merit any favor at His hand or claim a debt! When we have been employed in the duties of religious conversation, which will not excuse us from the exercises of devotion: when we have been *working for* God, still we must be *waiting on* God. Let us give Christ glory, let us attend Him with our praises, and then we shall eat and drink in the comfort of His love, and in this there is a feast!" [12]

We are often exhorted in the Word that we should not faint, be weary, or lazy, especially when it comes to our time with the Lord Nothing pierces my heart more than the account in the Garden of Gethsemane, when the disciples fall asleep during one of the

---

[12] Matthew Henry, *op. cit.* Volume 5, p. 765.

greatest spiritual battles ever fought, during our Lord's agony in the Garden.

And he cometh, and findeth them sleeping, and saith unto Peter, Simon, sleepest thou? Couldest not thou watch one hour? Watch ye and pray, lest ye enter into temptation. The spirit truly is ready, but the flesh is weak (Mark 14:37-38).

We were not there in the Garden, but how often have we grown weary, and fallen asleep in the midst of spiritual battles? The Bible warns us *therefore let us not sleep, as do others; but let us watch and be sober (1 Thessalonians 5:6),* but rather to *pray without ceasing (1 Thessalonians 5:17).*

The Devil knows the power of prayer, and he will do anything to stop us from communicating with our Heavenly Father. That is why Peter also warns us.

Be sober, be vigilant; because your adversary the devil, as a roaring lion, walketh about, seeking whom he may devour (1 Peter 5:8).

CHAPTER FOUR

OVERCOMING THE STRUGGLES

Let us not be weary in well doing: for in due season we reap,
if we faint not (Galatians 6:9).

If we are not spending quality time alone with the Lord, we are only living in survival mode. We may be able to deceive others, even ourselves, but we cannot deceive Him.

A few years ago we had a terrible drought during the summer, and I was so disappointed in the lack of roses in my rose garden. The plants looked healthy with shiny leaves but very few blossoms. The few that struggled to bloom produced such tiny roses they had no fragrance. I was sitting on my swing by the rose garden, where I have my time alone with the Lord, and He dropped this word into my heart:

> *Dear Child,*
> *Look at your rose garden! They look healthy enough yet nei-*
> *ther blossom nor give fragrance! Because of lack of water and*
> *the scorch of the sun they are in survival mode. They are do-*
> *ing all they can just to stay alive.*
> *My people stay too long in survival mode, and there is no*
> *fruit from their lives. Yes, they are spiritually alive and look*
> *and appear to be healthy, but where is the blossom and fra-*
> *grance from their lives? They are not drawing near and sup-*

ping with Me where I can give them rivers of living water to
sustain during all the trials of life.
Many will spend their lives at the Brazen Altar in survival
mode, where, yes, they are believers but are not disciples and
priests ministering unto Me. Only those committed to be
disciples can follow Me wherever I go, only they will follow
the Lamb wherever He goes.
Spend time daily and faithfully with Me that you may store
the hidden manna I will feed you daily, that you may have
some to give to others in the time of famine and drought.
Thereby your life will blossom and be a fragrance to Me.
Thus saith Papa.

I believe that the root of all excuses is a lack of spiritual appetite, due to a deficiency of gratitude, which will harden an indifferent heart. This lack of appetite will bring leanness to our souls and apathy of spirit. To have a healthy body we must eat food and drink. When we have no appetite, it is a warning sign that we are physically sick. If we continue down the road of not eating or drinking we would eventually die! I know that conclusion is not very profound, yet so many of us ignore this same warning sign in the spiritual realm, and then wonder why we have grown so cold and weak.

It has been said that we are what eat physically, but may I suggest that we are also what we eat spiritually. Many of us today are suffering from spiritual anorexia where the heavenly manna gets no further than our minds or at most we only chew it over due to a lack of appetite. While others are weak because of spiritual bulimia where we may swallow the word but it is thrown up because we do not obey it and appropriate it to our lives.

In order to overcome the struggles and excuses, we need to be hungry and thirsty for more of God. Not more knowledge, more study, more gifting, or even more ministry, but a deep hunger, that only fellowshipping with our Heavenly Father can satisfy. We must be as spiritually thirsty as a man who is desperately seeking water in a desert or he will die. If we are that thirsty and run after Him, He will quench our thirst with living water. *For he satisfieth the longing soul, and filleth the hungry soul with goodness (Psalm 107: 9).* We cannot be satisfied without a longing nor can we be filled except there be a hunger.

We can learn a lesson from two hungry souls who had an encounter with the Lord on the road to Emmaus after His resurrection.

But they constrained him, saying, Abide with us: for it is toward evening, and the day is far spent. And he went in to tarry with them. And it came to pass, as he sat at meat with them, he took bread, and blessed it, and brake, and gave to them. And their eyes were opened, and they knew him; and he vanished out of their sight (Luke 24: 29-31).

Not only did they invite Him, but the Word also tells us they compelled and begged Him to stay! They had a hungry desire that motivated them to want to spend time with Him. As He supped with them, He began to break bread and feed them, and instantly their eyes were opened and they knew Him. Similarly as we invite Him, with all our hearts, He will tarry with us, break bread (manna) for us and feed us. Then shall we see Him and know Him in the Word for we will then understand with spiritual insight.

> *Dear Child,*
> *Investment of time is needed for any intimate relationship!*
> *It will be a priority if it is important. You will always find*
> *the time to do what you really WANT TO; you will seldom*
> *find the time to do that which you feel you HAVE TO; in-*
> *stead you will find excuses! That is why it is not really a*
> *matter of time, it is a matter of motivation of the heart. That*
> *is why I continually remind you to have an appreciative*
> *heart for what I have done for you, then our time together*
> *will be out of the motivation of love and a "WANTING*
> *TO." Our relationship becomes lukewarm when you forget*
> *your beginnings.*
> *Thus saith Papa.*

How do we get to this place of WANTING TO rather than HAVING TO spend time with God? It is not a matter of willpower but rather love power! In His sovereignty God gave us the gift of free will to choose. Without that opportunity to choose we would not be accountable for our actions or choices. God wants us to surrender that free will back to Him in order that He may work in our lives, that we may truly pray:, "Not my will but thine be done" Only then can we claim: *for it is God which worketh in you both to will and to do of his good pleasure (Philippians 2:13).* Willpower will not keep us in fellowship with the Father only love for Him will keep us there.

80

WANTING TO is the result of a loving relationship, whereas HAVING TO is bringing us back under legal bondage.

> *Dear Child,*
> *A living sacrifice doesn't have to stay on the altar, as My Son didn't have to stay on the cross, except by cords of love! When you present yourself as a living sacrifice, it is only the motivation of love for Me that will keep you there.*
> *Regrets and 'should haves' will not secure you there. Good intentions will only slack the cords of love! Disobedience will break the cords of love!*
> *Only obedience will keep you secure in My presence, and will be a sweet savor. If you love Me keep My commandments.*
> *Thus saith Papa.*

A living sacrifice must be a WILLING sacrifice! Because a dead sacrifice has no choice!

It all comes down to a matter of choice. That choice will be based on motivation and priorities in our lives. We are not robots but creatures of free will to choose. God does not want the man He created to be like a machine, having no freedom of choice. But rather He wants a man who chooses to spend time with Him. God could have programmed us to obey and love Him, but this would not bring Him glory. Such obedience would have no spiritual value. There would be no fault or sin, yet neither would there be holiness, for obedience would be passive. God does not want automation. He wants a man with a free will who will choose to love and obey Him. I pray a desire will be ignited in our hearts to WANT to spend time with the Father. He does not want us to HAVE to spend time with Him, for 'HAVING TO' is the work of the flesh and that causes sweat, which is a stench to the Lord. The priest of Israel was commanded to wear only linen next his skin, not even a mixture of linen and wool was acceptable because the wool would cause sweat (Leviticus 6:10; 19:19). Remember God loves a cheerful giver, and that includes our time, only that given lovingly and cheerfully is a sweet fragrance to Him.

As I was meditating one day on the following scripture: *watch and pray, that ye enter not into temptation: the spirit indeed is willing, but the flesh is weak (Matthew 26:41),* I said this prayer:

> *Dear Father,*
> *Thank you for leading me to this scripture today, for no matter how I whip up my willpower to get it into shape to achieve spiritual ends, it always fails. I have to be carried on your power alone, Papa, help me grasp what this means, give me spiritual insight.*

He answered me:

> *Dear Child,*
> *Spiritual objectives can only be accomplished by spiritual power. Sweat is caused by the willpower trying to achieve something in the spiritual realm.*
> *Not only your talents and abilities must be brought under the subjection of the Holy Spirit but also surrender your*

82

willpower. It is not your willpower that must increase and become strong, it is the spirit that must increase over the flesh, which is the soul man, and the willpower is of the soul man.

My yoke is easy and My burden is light, come and learn of Me! You cannot beat the flesh into submission, you must deny the flesh and then it will die.

Be transformed by abiding in Me and learning of Me.

Die daily that I might live more in you!

Die daily that I might be resurrected in you!

Die daily that you might live forever!

Thus saith Papa.

So how do we bring the weak flesh into the submission of the spirit? The greatest willpower can only bring us to the point of willingness - no further! To be willing cannot give strength to the weak flesh! Something much more is needed. And Watchman Nee believes that "willpower is like a car without gas. It has to be pushed or towed. Left to itself it grinds to a halt. To trust to the human willpower for spiritual ends is therefore to encounter defeat. Spiritual power does not come from the human will, but from new life in Christ. This life provides another, deeper power beyond our volition, and by that power we find ourselves gloriously carried along in the Lord's victory!"[13] We must choose of our own free will to present ourselves as a living sacrifice. A living sacrifice? How can that be? Isn't that an oxymoron? As I reflected on this, the Lord dropped this prayer in my heart:

---

[13] Watchman Nee, *op. cit.*, Devotion May 15.

A living sacrifice,
Dying to self and alive to You.
In losing my life, I find it.
In dying, I live.
A living sacrifice,
Consume that which is not of You
Fill me with that which is of You.
Salt the sacrifice?
That I may thirst for more of You.

Within this prayer was not only the answer to my query, but also the key to a lack of appetite and thirst for God often experienced in our walk. The key was the "salting" of the sacrifice. In the Old Testament every sacrifice had to be salted.

And every oblation of thy meat offering shalt thou season with salt; neither shalt thou suffer the salt of the covenant of thy God to be lacking from thy meat offering: with all thine offerings thou shalt offer salt (Leviticus 2:13).

Jesus confirms this is necessary: *for every one shall be salted with fire, and every sacrifice shall be salted with salt (Mark 9:49).* That salt will cause such a desire and thirst for more of God; it will ignite a fire that will consume all that is not of Him. All that will be left will be His life in us. Only then will our living sacrifice be acceptable and pleasing in His sight, as an act of worship, for it will be a sweet savor unto Him. Salt may cause a wound or an offense to smart and hurt, but remember it will also cleanse it, thereby preserving our life.

We must die to our self-will by presenting ourselves daily as a living sacrifice, so that God may salt us, and we will have that thirst for more of Him:

Dear Child,
To learn My ways, you must hunger and thirst for righteousness, only then can My teachings quench that thirst and fill you to overflow. That thirsting is a result of My "salting" a yielded sacrifice. That "salting" may cause pain and a "smarting" in an open wound, but it will cleanse and heal, for remember I am the balm of Gilead. That thirsting caused by the "salting" can only be quenched by drinking in My ways, that will annihilate the flesh, but will satisfy the spirit.
Thus saith Papa.

Ungers Bible Dictionary states that "the meaning which the salt, with its power to strengthen the food and preserve it from corruption, imparted to the sacrifice was the unbending truthfulness of that self-surrender to the Lord embodied the sacrifice, by which all impurity and hypocrisy were repelled."

Surely the thirst for more of God created by the salt will save us from corruption and preserve us for Him. When we are thirsty, it will cause our roots to stretch and grow down deeper, to find that living water of life in the secret place, where we daily develop our secret history with God.

The Amplified Bible: The (Holy) Spirit and the bride (the church, the true Christians) say: *"Come! And let him who is listening say, Come! And let everyone who is thirsty (who is painfully conscious of his need of those things by which the soul is refreshed, supported and strengthened); and whoever earnestly desires to do it, let him come and take and appropriate (drink) the Water of Life without cost" (Revelation 22:17).*

> *Dear Child,*
> *Do you truly want to hear from Me? If you truly desire it… that is with all your heart you will hear My voice. Without obedience you will shy from My presence, and we will not have a harmonious relationship. Harmony comes from obedience to the Creator. All creation is in obedience to My purpose except mankind. Mankind has a choice, only man has that privilege, and that privilege can bring death or life. Walk in harmony with Me and find life.*
> *The Blood gives you the freedom to choose, and the Blood gives you the power to do what you know is right to do. You ask for help, the help is there paid for by the Blood, the door is open, the choice is yours, shake off the shackles and walk to freedom or sit in the prison of "I cannots" with broken chains still holding you captive. The choice is yours, Child, stay there, with the door of freedom wide open, or walk away into all you can be because of the price I paid. You are free, free, free! Body, soul and spirit. Live in the harmony of that freedom.*
> *Thus saith Papa.*

Today is the first day of the rest of your life. What will you do with it? What broken chains of excuses are still holding you captive from developing a secret history with God? Are you too busy? You cannot be bothered? You have left your first love? You don't truly believe you can fellowship with God? Are you living in the guilt of

86

unconfessed sin? Are you afraid of or discouraged by spiritual warfare? Have you grown weary or lazy? Whatever the excuse or whatever reason your mind can conceive, the door to overcome has been thrown open, to set you free that you might run to the loving arms of your Heavenly Father who wants to fellowship with you. The choice is yours!

Stand fast therefore in the liberty wherewith Christ hath made us free, and be not entangled again with the yoke of bondage (Galatians 5:1).

Dear Child,
The wall that will protect the treasure of this time with Me, is a boundary, a proactive boundary, and a habit, instituted from a decision of the will, to spend time with Me.
A conforming to this habit will be a wall of protection against other choices that would invade this precious time and steal from your spiritual life and growth. Beware of the enemy who will try to violate that boundary by laying many good choices before you. You know beforehand, the best use of your time is to spend it with Me lest you become lukewarm and a reproach.
Thus saith Papa.

Then said I unto them, Ye see the distress that we are in, how Jerusalem lieth waste, and the gates thereof are burned with fire: come, and let us build up the wall of Jerusalem, that we be no more a reproach (Nehemiah 2:17).

I wanted to close this chapter with a poem that says it all:

The Difference by Alan Grant[14]

I got up early one morning and rushed into the day,

---

[14] Alan Grant, "The Difference" Nittany Inspirations, 2009.

I had so much to accomplish that I didn't have time to pray.
Problems just tumbled about me, and heavier came each task.
Why doesn't God help me? I wondered He answered, "You didn't ask.
I wanted to see joy and beauty, but the day toiled on, gray and bleak,
I wondered why God didn't show me He said, "But you didn't seek."
I tried to come into God's presence, I used all my keys at the lock.
God gently and lovingly chided "My child you didn't knock."
I woke up early this morning, and paused before entering the day;
I had so much to accomplish that I had to take time to pray.

*In the day when I cried thou answeredst me, and strengthenedst
me with strength in my soul (Psalm 138:3).*

CHAPTER FIVE

WHAT IS PRAYER?

Call unto me, and I will answer thee, and shew thee great and mighty things, which thou knowest not (Jeremiah 33:3).

Prayer is communication with God, i.e. talking WITH God and not merely talking TO God. Prayer should be a dialogue not only a monologue because communication is not complete without a time to listen as well as a time to speak. Vines Bible Dictionary states that the verb form used for the word 'to pray' points back to the subject, in a reflexive sense, perhaps it emphasizes the part which the person praying has in his prayers. Also since the verb form can have a reciprocal meaning between the subject and object, it may emphasize the fact that prayer is basically communication, which always has to be two-way in order to be real.

We are apt to think it is a simple transaction! We ASK and God GIVES. Let us be careful least we seek only His hand and neglect to seek His Face. In our world today the art of communication is fast becoming a dying art form and our relationships are suffering. Is your relationship with God suffering because of lack of communica-tion with Him? Where is your prayer time on the following chart? It is not a matter of how long you spend with the Father, or how many words you say but rather the quality of that time and the level of the communication.

Communication Chart

Level 1 - Cliché conversation

Level 2 - Reporting facts about others

Level 3 - My ideas and judgments

Level 4 - My feelings and emotions

Level 5 - Peak communication/total personal honesty

Level 1 Cliché: "How are you?" Reply: "oh, I'm fine!" No personal sharing, each person remains safely behind his screen.

Level 2 Facts: Content to tell what someone else has said, but offer no personal commentary on these facts.

Level 3 Ideas: What we think. This is where real conversation begins. Step out of solitary confinement and risk sharing some of our own ideas and decisions. Still cautious and if we sense what we are saying is not being accepted or really listened to we will retreat.

Level 4 Feelings: Sharing the feelings or emotions behind the ideas.

Level 5 Peak: Personal honesty/all deep relationships especially marriage must be based on absolute openness and honesty with hearts totally naked. Not many are willing to step up to this level because this level could involve the risk of rejection. We should not fear this level with our Heavenly Father for He knows us the best and yet He still loves us the most.

If you do spend time in prayer each day, what is the level of that communication?

When we pray and talk with God are we really totally honest about ourselves, investing quality time with Him? Or do we cop out by offering a shallow cliché prayer of 'Bless this day and bless my family'? Are we only comfortable stepping up to level 2 where we merely talk to God about others, keeping our own hearts safely behind a screen? We have an example of this from the Word in John chapter 4, where Jesus encounters the Samaritan woman at the well. Jesus wanted to talk with her about her own condition, but all she wanted to talk about was the facts concerning the difference between Jews and Samaritans. Even after Jesus revealed her past to her, she still continued on the Level 2 of communication where she only wanted to talk about the facts of where Samaritans worship and where Jews say you should worship.

We have yet another example in Jesus' conversation with his disciples in Matthew chapter 16, where He inquires of His disciples at level 2 " Who do others say that I am?" However Jesus takes the conversation a level deeper to level 3 by asking them "Whom do you say that I am?" Have the confidence to step up to a deeper level because God has promised He will hear your cry and He will never reject an honest, open heart.

Dear Child,

Confidence comes from spending time with Me. As you spend time with Me you grow to know Me better, and as you know Me better, you have confidence in your relationship with Me. Carnal confidence is the fruit of pride, spiritual confidence is the fruit of true humility, gained by recognizing your inadequacy while you are in My presence. Your confidence is not in self but rather in your relationship to Me. Be bold, be strong, for the Lord your God is with you! Thus saith Papa.

Just as in all relationships, when you spend time talking with someone, you learn to trust that person more because you are gaining confidence in the relationship. It is no less in our relationship to our heavenly Papa. In our quiet time do we do all the talking or do we sometimes just sit and listen for His voice? Do we know and understand His voice above other voices? (See chapter on "How do I hear His Voice?").

You only get to know a person when you get to know their heart. This takes investment of time and deep communication. Do you want to know the Father's heartbeat? I want to interject a personal story here to help us understand this better: during the months I was in and out of sinus rhythm with my heart, my husband grew sensitive to the sound of my heartbeat as he would put his ear on my chest and just listen, and he would know instinctively if my heart was out of rhythm or normal. We had medical instruments that could measure that for us, but John just knew without that aid, by spending much time alone with me and learning to be sensitive to the sound of my heart beating.

You must spend time alone with Him and talk with Him intimately to grow sensitive to His heartbeat. You cannot hear anyone's heartbeat from afar off, you must spend time close to them. He already knows your heart better than you know it yourself but He wants you to know His heartbeat. From this time you will gain confidence in your relationship to the Father. It is not only a time of communication but also a time of sweet fellowship.

From Genesis to Revelation God is seeking to have fellowship with us.

And they heard the voice of the Lord God walking in the garden in the cool of the day: and Adam and his wife hid themselves from the presence of the Lord God amongst the trees of the garden. And the Lord God called unto Adam, and said unto him, Where art thou? And he said, I heard thy voice in the garden, and I was afraid, because I was naked; and I hid myself (Genesis 3:8-9).

Behold, I stand at the door, and knock: if any man hear my voice, and open the door, I will come in to him, and will sup with him, and he with me (Revelation 3:20).

Man was created in God's image that man might have the capacity to fellowship with God. That fellowship was broken in the Garden because the image was marred and defaced due to sin. The good news of the gospel is that our fellowship can now be restored because of the blood of our Sacrificial Lamb, which washes away our sin, making it possible for man to be conformed to His image once again. In the Garden He called, "Adam where are you?" Do you hear Him calling you? He already knows where you are but he wants you to be searching for Him that you may have fellowship together. God wants to communicate and fellowship with You!

I do not intend to limit the subject of prayer to the intimate fellowship I'm writing about in this book. There are many great books out there on other aspects of prayer, such as the topic of intercessory prayer or how to get your prayers answered. I would never only confine prayer to the topic of this book. Our almighty God can talk to us anywhere, anytime and anyway He so chooses. He will and can choose any window to our soul to get our attention, be it through another person, circumstances, movies, books, music or anything in our everyday life. Surely if God can use an ass and speak through an ass (Numbers 22:23-35) He can speak through anything or anyone. I am writing about a hidden fellowship and conversation with God, that will develop an intimate relationship with Him, which will ultimately cultivate a deep, healthy spiritual root structure in the True Vine. The purpose of this precious prayer time is to mature us, change our hearts, transform our thinking and mold us to His image. It is a daily divine appointment to visit the Potter's house as Jeremiah the prophet wrote about: *arise, and go down to the potter's house, and there I will cause thee to hear my words. Then I went down to the potter's house, and, behold, he wrought a work on the wheels. And the vessel that he made of clay was marred in the hand of the potter: so he*

made it again another vessel, as seemed good to the potter to make it
(Jeremiah 18:2-4).

As we devote time to develop a secret history with God, we will grow accustom to not only know His heart, but also know His voice. We will have fine tuned our spiritual radio to instinctively recognize His voice in our everyday walk.

> *Dear Child,*
> *Without time alone with Me, you do not have an intimate relationship with Me. You may have a personal relationship but not an intimate one. Intimacy is only acquired in a place of solitude, stillness and total honesty; nothing kept back with total surrender.*
> *This requires a desire to be with Me, greater than any other desire, and the yielding of your will and agenda, with your life and heart totally uncovered and naked before Me.*
> *Thus saith Papa.*

This is the place of the highest communication with the Father, the place of intimacy.

What is prayer?

Prayer is something that has no human or earthly substitute.

Prayer is intimacy with God!

> *He shall call upon me, and I will answer him*
> *(Psalm 91:15).*

CHAPTER SIX

HOW DO I HEAR HIS VOICE?

*Arise, and go down to the potter's house, and there I will
cause thee to hear my words (Jeremiah 18:2).*

Jesus promised us in John 10:27 that *"My sheep hear My voice..."*
and yet many sheep wonder why they do not hear His Voice. Do I
have a formula to insure you will hear His voice? No, I do not, but
I can share with you what I have learned to cause my heart to be
more sensitive to that still small voice. I believe I have learned
scriptural conditions to meet this promise. Along with every
promise in the Word are conditions, and no less with this promise
that His sheep will hear His voice. We must approach our communion with the Lord:

1. With a pure, clear conscience,
2. In confident faith that He will speak to us,
3. With an attentive ear listening in silent anticipation.

To help us understand I'm going to use an analogy of a radio
transmission. The Webster's Dictionary defines a radio as "the wireless transmission and reception of electric impulses or signals by
means of electric waves, and the use of these waves for that wireless

transmission of the electric impulses into which sound is converted."

I'm also reminded of the lyrics of the old country song "Turn your radio on."

> "Don't you know that everybody is a radio receiver
> All you gotta do is listen for the call
> Get in touch with God - turn your radio on."[15]

In the world of radio there are many radio wave frequencies, there is AM/FM/VHF, etc. To find the station you are looking for, you need to tune your radio to the right radio wave frequency. The airwaves are so sensitive that if you are not tuned in right on the spot, there will be static or interferences blocking your reception. To be fine-tuned right on the station you will have to tune out unwanted stations. So always remember that the quality of the reception depends on the receiver. How do we tune into God's wave band without static or interference from other voices? How do we hear and recognize His voice above other voices out there? The Lord promises that we will not only hear His voice, but that we will know it is His voice.

> *And when he putteth forth his own sheep, he goeth before them, and the sheep follow him: for they know his voice. And a stranger will they not follow, but will flee from him: for they know not the voice of strangers (John 10:4-5).*

---

[15] Lyrics from Roy Acuff, "Turn Your Radio On".

1) A pure, clear conscience

I believe that the conscience is the wave band frequency for the voice of the spirit. That is why it is so important to keep our conscience clear or we will get static on the line. Vines Bible Dictionary defines the conscience "as that faculty by which we apprehend the will of God, as that which is designed to govern our lives." There are many voices out there clamoring for our attention, even within our own being. The voice of our body is our feelings, the voice of our mind is our reasoning, but only the conscience is the avenue for the voice of the spirit. Feelings do not tend to be a good indicator of the difference between right and wrong. From start to finish the Christian experience is a journey of faith. We live by faith not by joy. Joy is wonderful, but it feeds our sensations and lures us into seeking the things above only at times of excitement. Then should our blissful feelings cease our interest wanes. That is not the walk of faith. Our feelings are always changing. He is the same God every day, be it cloudy or sunny. Are we trusting in the up-and-down existence of our feelings, or is our faith anchored in the Unchanging One? Feelings belong to the soulish realm not the spiritual.

Can we then trust the voice of the mind, which is our reasoning, more than our feelings? No, because the mind will always somehow justify what the heart has already chosen to do.

Dear Child,
Listen, listen for the voice of the Spirit, be aware of the
urging of the Holy Spirit, and obey immediately, lest you
think about it, and the voice of reason, doubt and fear
takeover and drowns out My voice.
Thus saith Papa.

Jimmy Cricket from the book *Pinocchio* said it well: "always let your conscience be your guide." The conscience, which is part of our innermost being and spirit will never lead us astray or away from God's will for us. Our conscience is such a sensitive and intricate part of our being, that the New Testament gives no less than thirty exhortations and warnings concerning our conscience, because this part of our being is so instrumental in our relationship to God and our spiritual growth.

Jesus warns us: *the eye is the lamp of the body. So, if your eye is sound, your entire body will be full of light; but if your eye is unsound, your whole body will l be full of darkness. If then the very light in you (your conscience) is darkened, how dense is that darkness (Matthew 6:22-23 - Amplified translation).* The 'eye' in this passage refers to our conscience, which is to the soul, as the eye is to the body, to guide and direct our motions.

Vines Bible Dictionary explains that the word for 'light' in this same passage, "is used metaphorically of ethical qualities here, because primarily light is a luminous emanation probably of force from certain bodies, which enables the eye to discern form and color. Light requires an organ adapted for its reception. According to Matthew 6:22 the eye is the organ for the body to receive light, and metaphorically the conscience is the organ for the inner man to receive light. Where the eye is absent, or where it has become impaired from any cause, light is useless. Man is incapable of receiving spiritual light inasmuch as he lacks the capacity for spiritual things."

But the natural man receiveth not the things of the Spirit of God: for they are foolishness unto him: neither can he know them, because they are spiritually discerned (1 Corinthians 2:14).

Hence believers are called "the sons of light" in Luke 16:8, not merely because they have received a revelation from God, but because in the New Birth they received the spiritual capacity. The 'conscience' is now restored to the 'God consciousness' it had before the fall.

Dear Child,
Filter your actions and words through your conscience and you will be led by My Spirit. Don't act or speak based only on feelings or reasoning, be led by the inner man not the mind or the flesh. The arm of flesh will fail you and the mind is being transformed, only the inner man is born of Me and knows Me and knows My voice. It was the inner man that responded to my invitation of grace on the day of your visitation.
Thus saith Papa.

We now have an organ adapted for the reception of the light of God's voice.

Matthew Henry's commentary explains it so well from the following scripture: *and though the Lord give you the bread of adversity, and the water of affliction, yet shall not thy teachers be removed into a corner any*

101

more, but thine eyes shall see thy teachers. And thine ears shall hear a word behind thee, saying, This is the way, walk ye in it, when ye turn to the right hand, and when ye turn to the left (Isaiah 30:20-21).

> It is promised that they shall have the benefit, not only of the public ministry, but of private and particular admonition and advice (Isaiah 30:21): 'Thy ears shall hear a word behind thee.' Whence this word shall come from behind you, from someone whom you don't see, but who sees you! 'Thine eyes see thy teachers' but this is a teacher out of sight, it is thine own conscience, which shall now by the grace of God be awakened to do its office. 'This is the way, walk ye in it' When you are doubting, conscience will direct you the way of duty; When you are dull of hearing and weary, conscience will quicken you in the way.[16]

How do we hear the voice of the Lord? We hear His Voice through the avenue of our conscience. As God has not left Himself without witness, so He has not left us without guides to show us our way. The checks of the conscience and the strivings of God's spirit will set us right and prevent us from going astray, if we listen to that still, small voice.

Dear Child,

Fine tune your conscience by keeping it clear, that you might discern good and evil, that spiritually you may see black and white, and not stumble over gray. The gray muddies the water and will confuse you and cause you to stumble. Gray will cause the voice of the conscience to grow softer. Don't justify gray, let your "yea" be "yea" and your "nay" be "nay". Don't justify actions and words with the reasoning of the mind, so that you can live with yourself,

---

[16] Matthew Henry, *op. cit.,* Volume 4, p. 170.

because this will cause the flesh to be fed and thrive, but will quench and grieve the spirit.
Thus saith Papa.

Which show the work of the law written in their hearts, their conscience also bearing witness (Romans 2:15).

The Spirit itself beareth witness with our spirit, that we are the children of God (Romans 8:16).

I say the truth in Christ, I lie not, my conscience also bearing me witness in the Holy Ghost (Romans 9:1).

What does it really mean to 'Bear witness with our spirits?' 'Beareth witness' in all these three passages is the Greek word *'Summartureo'*. These are the only three times that this word is used in the Scriptures. Therefore somehow these three verses explain each other. Surely our conscience plays an important role in this process, and our conscience is a channel for the voice of God through the Holy Spirit. It is in our conscience that we know that we know! If we could only train ourselves to always listen to our conscience we would know the right choice to make. For when we are listening to our conscience we are hearing the spirit.

God has spoken to His children in times past, and we hear echoes of His voice in the Scriptures as He spoke to Moses or to David, but we long to hear Him speaking to us directly, personally and intimately.

Let us draw near with a true heart in full assurance of faith, having our hearts sprinkled from an evil conscience, and our bodies washed with pure water (Hebrews 10:22).

Dear Child,

Do you truly want to hear from Me? If you truly desire it, that is, with all your heart, you will hear my voice. Without obedience you will shy from my presence, and we will not have a harmonious relationship. Harmony comes from obedience to the Creator. All creation is in obedience to my purpose except mankind. Mankind has a choice, only man has that privilege, and that privilege can bring death or life. Walk in harmony with Me and find life.

Thus saith Papa.

Running from God because of a guilty conscience is as old as the Garden of Eden. God would fellowship with Adam and Eve in the cool of the day, but on the day that they were disobedient, guilt set in and they hid from God. He is calling to you today just as He did in the Garden, "Child, where are you?" The Father wants to restore that Garden fellowship with each of His children and He doesn't want guilt to cause you to shy from His presence. He has provided a way to cleanse your conscience that this fellowship may be restored. Therapists and counselors can talk through your problems, give advice and maybe even help you to live with what you have done, but no therapist or counselor can cleanse your conscience of guilt. God is the only counselor who can cleanse that guilt and wash away that sin in the Blood of Jesus that your conscience may be a clear, pure channel to commune with the Father. What voice does God use to convict you when you have been disobedient? He convicts you through your conscience.

And they which heard it, being convicted by their own conscience (John 8:9).

The result of restored fellowship will depend on your response to that voice of conviction. Will you try to justify it with the reasoning voice of the mind? Will you ignore it because the voice of the body says: 'I don't feel like dealing with it'? Or will you try to drown it out by running from God and trying to fill your life with the busyness of this world? Or will you respond by running to the arms of a loving Heavenly Father, repentantly seeking His forgiveness, that your communion with Him may be restored.

Come now, and let us reason together, saith the Lord: though your sins be as scarlet, they shall be as white as snow; though they be red like crimson, they shall be as wool (Isaiah 1:18).

If our heart's desire is to have an intimate relationship with the Father and to clearly hear His voice, we must daily ask Him: *search me, O God, and know my heart: try me, and know my thoughts. And see if there be any wicked way in me, and lead me in the way everlasting (Psalm 139:23-24).* Our conscience is the candle of the Lord to search our hearts. *The spirit of man is a candle of the Lord, searching all the inward parts of the belly (Proverbs 20:27).* We must then look into the mirror of the Word and cleanse ourselves if there is a blemish on our conscience. This is why God gives us the applicable type of the Brazen Laver in the Outer Court of the Tabernacle. The Brazen

Laver, which was lined in mirrors and full of water, speaks of self-judgment, and it was placed right outside the Holy Place. The priests would look into the mirrored Laver to examine themselves for dust and dirt, which they had picked up during their walk in the Outer Court, which is a type of the world. This was God's provision for them to cleanse themselves before entering His Presence to fellowship and minister unto Him.

> *I pray not that thou shouldest take them out of the world, but that thou shouldest keep them from the evil. They are not of the world, even as I am not of the world. Sanctify them through thy truth: thy word is truth (John 17:15-17).*

We may not be of this world, but we can become tainted during our walk in the world. God has also provided a Laver for us, it is the Word of truth. Likewise we must also wash off the contamination of our walk in the Outer Court, if we wish to press on in to commune with the Father in the Holy Place.

Paul warns us: *having faith and a good conscience. By rejecting conscience, certain persons have suffered shipwreck in the faith (1 Timothy1:19).* This is explained by Watchman Nee: "a ship which is wrecked cannot sail. Whether a Christian can proceed with his service for God depends therefore on whether he has any offense outstanding on his conscience. Confession to God will remove the offense; but as long as the believer accepts the accusation of Satan, his conscience is stuck with it. He cannot effectively serve God until his conscience is at rest once again."[17]

---

[17] Watchman Nee, *op. cit.*, Devotion March 7.

2) Confident Faith

If I regard iniquity in my heart, the Lord will not hear me (Psalm 66:18).

But if our conscience is void of offense toward God and man, we will then have the confident faith to commune with the Father, believing that He not only will hear our cry but will also answer us. We are taught in Romans 10:17 that *faith cometh by hearing, and hearing by the word of God.* Therefore we can build our faith to be both heard and answered from the following promises:

> *The eyes of the Lord are upon the righteous, and his ears are open unto their cry (Psalm 34:15).*

> *Call unto me, and I will answer thee, and show thee great and mighty things, which thou knowest not (Jeremiah 33:3).*

We receive all the promises of God by faith, no less the promise that we can commune with our Heavenly Father.

> *But without faith it is impossible to please him: for he that cometh to God must believe that he is, and that he is a rewarder of them that diligently seek him (Hebrews 11:6).*

Thus we must believe that we will hear His voice. A clear conscience will give us that confidence.

> *Beloved, if our heart condemn us not, then have we confidence toward God. And whatsoever we ask, we receive of him, because we keep his commandments, and do those things that are pleasing in his sight (1 John 3:21-22).*

As we humbly confess our need of cleansing we will have assurance of acceptance by faith in His blood to draw near. Instead, we often stand afar, because our confidence in our relationship to our heavenly Papa is shaken due to unconfessed sin. If your conscience is clear before God, do not let the enemy rob you of the joy of your salvation, which is an intimate relationship with Him. If there is an outstanding offense on your conscience, confess it to God, that the enemy may not have a hold over you. When you clear your conscience your heart will no longer condemn you, and you will once more have that confident faith to draw near. But remember even with confident faith we must come in humble boldness because boldness without humility is only arrogance!

3) Listen in silent anticipation

And they heard the voice of the Lord God walking in the garden in the cool of the day (Genesis 3:8).

Behold, I stand at the door, and knock: if any man hear my voice, and open the door, I will come in to him, and will sup with him, and he with me (Revelation 3:20).

Since the Bible confirms from Genesis to Revelation that we were created to have fellowship with God, prayer should not be limited to a monologue, but rather was intended to be a dialogue. Communication consists of a time to talk and a time to listen. It should be no different in our communication with God. We talk to God and He listens to our cry. He answers our cry and we listen. This was the part that was missing in my time with God. I needed to learn to be still and just listen.

Dear Child,

I formed you in your mother's womb. I formed your heart and I can form the words in that heart. Come apart to hear those words.

In solitude and stillness you must have a listening ear, not just a hearing ear.

A listening ear is anticipating and active, but a hearing ear is only reacting to the noise of sound in a passive mode!

A listening ear anticipates in faith from within!

A hearing ear responds to noise from without!

Shut out the world and be still, listening in anticipation in confident faith that I am a rewarder of those who diligently seek My face.

Thus saith Papa.

Be still, and know that I am God (Psalm 46:10).

Hear, O Lord, when I cry with my voice: have mercy also upon me, and answer me (Psalm 27:7).

Listening – is the expectation of hearing/ to make an effort to hear something/to hear what is said with attention/ to give ear to/ to tune in.

Hearing – is the process, function or power of perceiving sound/ special sense by which noises and tones are received as stimuli/ ears are the organ for hearing.

There are sounds and noises all around us in everyday life which we hear passively but we are not actively listening to them. The CONSCIENCE is the organ (ears) for hearing the voice of the Spirit. BUT we must be LISTENING in expectation.

Now there are even days when I have no monologue of words to offer, no 'to do' list to offer, nor 'grocery list' of requests. I am learning that some days I need to just sit motionless and silent on the Potter's wheel, where He will cause me to hear His voice.

Arise, and go down to the potter's house, and there I will cause thee to hear my words (Jeremiah 18:2).

Our God is not impassive toward us like an unresponsive pagan idol, for as we read in Psalm 135:16-17: *idols have ears but cannot hear and mouths but cannot speak!*

> *Dear Child,*
> *There are many avenues, which I use to communicate with you, but nothing will ever replace that still small voice. Listen! Listen! Be still and know that I am God. Not the Scriptures, not the law, not doctrine, but I am God! All the above is only relevant as you hear My voice.*
> *Thus saith Papa.*

Yes, of course, we need to study and read the Scriptures, but not at the neglect of fellowshipping and talking with our Father. As we meditate on the Scriptures, it not only gives us direction, wisdom, correction, and encouragement but above all else it reveals the heart of our Father that we might recognize His voice as we communicate with Him. Yes, we need to work and minister for God in the Outer Court, but not at the neglect of ministering to God in the Holy Place.

As I have stated before and I believe it is worth repeating. When religion has its last word, there is little that we need other than God Himself. Remembering the words of the ancient Westminster cate- chism which reads: "What is the chief end of man? Man's chief end is to glorify God and enjoy Him forever."[18]

Tozer writes in his book *Pursuit of God*: "quietness of the soul, the fruit of truly seeking God, is seldom found in this century. Far too many have come to accept turbulence of the soul as the norm and have ceased to seek God with their whole hearts. Some have even fled the cities to the suburbs and country in the hope of finding this quietness, only to discover their hearts still restless."[19]

Oh! That we would see that sitting still in solitude and quietness before the Lord will give us such confidence in our relationship to our Father. This confidence will be our strength according to Isaiah 30:7: *their strength is to sit still.* And, *for thus saith the Lord GOD, the Holy One of Israel; in returning and rest shall ye be saved; in quietness and in confidence shall be your strength (Isaiah 30:15)*

Herod inquired of the scribes the place of the Messiah's birth. In Matthew 2:5 they gave Herod the correct answer. But they didn't go themselves to seek Him, instead they went back to their books! It is not enough to know the Word we must also know the Author! Even understanding the Word is not sufficient if it doesn't lead us to know God! The knowledge of the scribes could have led them to

---

[18] Thomas Vincent, *op. cit.*

[19] A.W. Tozer, "The Pursuit of God," Christian Publications, 1982, p. 3.

see and know the Messiah when He was born in Bethlehem, but they did err not knowing the Spirit of the Word. Reading and learning the Scriptures must do more than cause us to be Bible literate, it must lead us to know the Father. "Today we need prophets not scribes, for the scribe tells you what he has read, while the prophet tells you what he has heard! We are overrun today with orthodox scribes, but where are the prophets?"[20]

Spiritual things are spiritually discerned and as with all things even in the physical realm, it takes time and experience to develop sensitivity. We all know that the more time we spend talking with someone, the more we grow to recognize not only their voice but also the content of their conversation and their temperament, motivation and character. Have you ever received a report of words supposed to have been said by someone you know very well, and the words just sound out of character? Or when you read between the lines, it is not the motivation of the person you know so well? The familiar sound of that person's voice is not the only confirmation to recognize their voice. The same is true when we are learning to be sensitive to the voice of the Lord:

- You learn to recognize His voice by the content; does it line up with the written Word? God will never contradict His Word.

- You learn to recognize His voice by the temperament; does it impart peace or confusion and stress to your heart?

---

[20] A. W. Tozer, *Ibid.*, p. 41.

- You learn to recognize His voice by the motivation; does it bring conviction or does it bring condemnation? Does it bring healing or accusation?

- You learn to recognize His voice by His character; does it instill the assurance of love, acceptance and hope, or does it instill fear, rejection and hopelessness?

Ken Gire's book *Windows of the Soul* has to be one of my favorite writings and has truly impacted my being. Ken states in the book: "whenever He succeeds in reaching us, a window opens between heaven and earth in a moment of revelation. We are offered words of guidance and correction. Words of wisdom and understanding. Words of forgiveness and assurance. Words that our soul hungers for. 'Man shall not live by bread alone but by every word that proceeds from the mouth of God.' If this is true our very lives depend upon those words. They are in fact the daily bread of our soul."[21]

Listen, listen, do you hear Him knocking? In faith reply: *Speak, Lord; for thy servant heareth (1 Samuel 3:9)*. It is a remarkable fact that sheep and pets unerringly recognize the voice of their master. There is voice recognition in nature.

The ox knows its owner, and the donkey its master's crib; but Israel does not know, my people do not understand (Isaiah 1:3).

It is in Satan's best interest to make an inherent mystery of God's word coming directly to the individual believer.

How can we distinguish the voice of God from our own subconscious? E. Stanley Jones says: "perhaps the rough distinction is

---

[21] Ken Gire, *Windows of the Soul*, Zondervan Publishing House, 1996.

this: The voice of the subconscious argues with you, tries to convince you; but the inner voice of God does not argue, does not try to convince you. It just speaks, and it is self – authenticating."[22] When Jesus spoke, his words had a weight of authority that opened up the understanding of his hearers and created faith in them.

For he taught them as one having authority, and not as the scribes (Matthew 7:29).

His voice bears authority within itself it doesn't need to be loud or hysterical.

I first became aware of the inspiration that God was impressing upon my heart by the effect it was having in my life. It was a living word because it was bearing fruit and changing me from the inside out. Then when God would impress upon me to share one of my hidden manna devotions with someone, it was often in fear and trembling that I would venture out and obey, but it was always "a word in season for that person."

A word spoken in due season, how good is it! (Proverbs 15:23).

These precious words were not only changing me from the inside out but others as well.

Adele Rogers St. John remarks (perhaps somewhat overconfidently but yet to the point): "the first time you receive guidance you will

---

[22] E. Stanley Jones, quote from *Wasting Time With God: A Christian Spirituality of Friendship With God* by Klaus Issler, Intervarsity Press, 2001.

114

know the difference. You can mistake rhinestones for diamonds but you can never mistake a diamond for a rhinestone."

God will speak to you in a language you will understand. He wants you to know His will for you.

Do not be conformed to this world, but be transformed by the renewing of your minds, so that you may discern what is the will of God - what is good and acceptable and perfect (Romans 12:2).

Wherefore be ye not unwise, but understanding what the will of the Lord is (Ephesians 5:17).

The language the Lord uses to speak to me is through the passion and understanding I have for the Tabernacle, or through my love for gardening. For you it will be where you have understanding and passion. Why would He try to communicate to you through a language you don't understand? Remember how Jesus taught through parables. He used farming, fishing or sheep farming. He knew this would make His teaching not only applicable but also understandable to those who had an ear to hear.

We must have our hearts fixed that we will invest this precious time with the Father. Consistency leads to habit forming. Habit forming leads to doing something naturally, even without programming it. They say if you consistently do something for 21 days, it will become a habit, it will be in your brain computer.

We enter the gate with thanksgiving and gratitude. We lift up holy hands that have been washed at the Laver. And we boldly yet with humility, because our feet still walk on the dust of the earth, enter His presence, where spiritually we are seated in heavenly places in Christ Jesus (Ephesians 2:6). It is a journey we must make alone to have intimate fellowship with Papa.

It is a pilgrimage we make alone each day with a clear conscience, confident faith and an anticipating, listening ear to hear from Papa.

> *"Come, go down to the potter's house, and there I will let you hear my words." So I went down to the potter's house, and there he was working at his wheel. The vessel he was making of clay was spoiled in the potter's hand, and he reworked it into another vessel, as seemed good to him (Jeremiah 18:2-4).*

These precious words from Papa will not only encourage, exhort, warn, and reveal His will for you, BUT will change you! He will be changing you from the inside out, working daily on your innermost being, conforming you to His image, as He reworks on you to make you a vessel of honor.

Speak, Lord; for thy servant heareth (1 Samuel 3:9).

CHAPTER SEVEN

JOURNALIZING

Thus speaketh the Lord God of Israel, saying, Write thee all the words that I have spoken unto thee in a book (Jeremiah 30:2).

We hear a lot today about journalizing and the stores are full of journals to fit every taste and need. People keep journals for many different reasons. Some do it just to have an account of their day, while others use them as a record of their experiences, ideas or reflections. I keep my daily journal as a record of my secret time alone with God. Journalizing is as old as King David. If he hadn't recorded his secret time alone with God, we would not have the book of Psalms.

Several years ago as I was reflecting on the substance and quality of my devotional time, the Holy Spirit illuminated a missing component in that devotional time. I was studying and meditating on the Word and I was offering God my thanksgiving and my prayer requests. I was even sometimes keeping a record of my prayer requests so that I could later enter the date the request was answered. But the vital missing component was a quiet time when I was still and silent enough to hear His voice. In our hectic, noisy, busy world it is so hard to just sit still without letting our thoughts wander or even fall asleep. I questioned, "Lord, you just want me to sit still and do nothing?" This is so inconceivable in our multi-task and goal oriented society, with not enough hours in the day to fulfill our many roles and commitments. At least if I am studying the Word, or offering prayers, I am being productive but to be still and do nothing was such an extravagant waste of my time, I reasoned. He told me:

> *Dear Child,*
> *Take time to spend with Me! As you behold Me you will become more like Me! Take time to listen! Learn to know My voice, learn to discern My voice, your spirit will bear witness that it is My voice. My voice is not in the wind or the thunderstorm but it is that still small voice, be still and know that I am God.*
> *It's in stillness that you enter My presence, that's why I speak to you in a still small voice, so that you will have to come apart and stop! And think only on Me.*
> *Thus saith Papa.*

When I learned to yield not only myself but also my time to the Lord, I began to understand the purpose of those few still moments. I prayed:

> *During these quiet moments of intimacy with You each day, the stresses and cares of this world seem so insignificant, as I spend some time with You in your time zone of eternity. Help me today to redeem my time and be a wise servant*

during my pilgrim walk in the earthly time zones that I am
restricted to.

The Lord exhorted me with this word:

Child,
In eternity there is no time, and therefore no time limits or
deadlines, there is only eternity. Only in earthly time zones
are there limits and deadlines to meet, which brings stresses
and anxiety. Through this testing, child, learn the lessons of
balance, responsibility and priority. Learn to live according
to eternity and keep your spiritual eyes on the "big picture"
and fix your heart on Me, for only I am Alpha and Omega,
the first and the last, the beginning and the end. There is
nothing of worth outside of Me, there is nothing of value
outside of eternity.
Thus saith Papa.

Sooner or later we all need to take an account of our time, which after all is our life. Are we wasting it, spending it, or investing it? If we are wasting our time we are spilling out our lives without any purpose. If we are spending our time we are often only reaping momentary pleasures. But if we invest our time wisely, with a view of eternity, we will not only reap a reward in the life to come, but will receive an interest on that time invested and will have more time. I don't know how it works but I always have more time when I invest that time in quietness before God. After we have given God a tithe of our time, we will discover that we will accomplish much more with the remaining nine-tenths.

Child,
Daily invest that time alone with Me. It will reap a vast return. By investing time, you will have interest on that time, and therefore have more time. I have abundant time, I am eternity, the beginning and the end.
Thus saith Papa.

How difficult it is in our over active lives to come to a stop! Not just to stop our world and activities, but to find a quiet corner for stillness of mind, to meditate only on the moment without thoughts straying. At that moment of desperately searching for an answer to the dilemma I found the solution. If I would commit to write the words that My heavenly Papa was speaking to my heart, during that time of stillness, my thoughts would not wander. I remember reading about the life of Saint Patrick, who would stand in a cold creek in the early morning, so he would not fall asleep during his quiet time with God. I don't know about you, but I would rather journal than have to stand in a cold creek to keep me attentive and awake.

This is where faith is needed to start to write even if it is only a few words, let it flow, don't stop to think, for then we would be listening to the voice of reason, instead of the voice of the spirit. Let it bypass the seat of the soul which is our mind, as we would while praying in the spirit. When God reaches our spirit, whether it be by illumination of the written Word or by a personal word dropped in our hearts, it must be clothed in faith to have life, otherwise it is only a dry empty husk of a seed with no life.

For unto us was the gospel preached, as well as unto them: but the word preached did not profit them, not being mixed with faith in them that heard it (Hebrews 4:2).

Take another leap of faith and write it in the first person. I've had those I've ministered to in this area, who are more comfortable with writing, "I think or I believe that God is saying so and so to me." After a few weeks of growing in faith in this area, they are so excited when they finally write it in the first person. As I read over my journals of the past ten years, I saw how my faith had grown, since it had taken me almost a year before I began to journalize in the first person. And then it took several months before I had the faith to step out and seal my writing with "Thus saith Papa." This stopped the enemy in his tracks, before he could challenge my faith, by sowing a thought of skepticisms that I had actually heard God's voice, and thereby abort the life of the seed that God had just planted in my heart. If he fails to shake my faith in this area, he will then instead try to distort the words that God had spoken to me, just as he distorted God's word to Adam and Eve.

Now the serpent was more subtil than any beast of the field which the Lord God had made. And he said unto the woman, Yea, hath God said, Ye shall not eat of every tree of the garden? And the woman said unto the serpent, We may eat of the fruit of the trees of the garden: But of the fruit of the tree which is in the midst of the garden, God hath said, Ye shall not eat of it, neither shall ye touch it, lest ye die. And the serpent said unto the woman, Ye shall not surely die: For God doth know that in the day ye eat thereof, then your eyes shall be opened, and ye shall be as gods, knowing good and evil (Genesis 3-5). (See chapter on "How do I Hear His Voice?").

I use the word 'Papa' when referring to My Heavenly Father based on the Greek word 'Abba' from Romans 8:15: *for ye have not received the spirit of bondage again to fear; but ye have received the Spirit of adoption, whereby we cry, Abba, Father.* Also, as we learn in Galatians 4:6, *and because ye are sons, God hath sent forth the Spirit of his Son into your hearts, crying, Abba, Father.* Vines Bible Dictionary defines 'Abba' as the word framed by the lips of infants and betokens unreasoning trust. A Greek infant's first formation of our English 'Dada', very often the first word a child speaks.

As I am still before God and listen I frame those special intimate moments with words, because as a Chinese Proverb puts it, "the palest ink lasts longer than the strongest memory." I believe that as I am journalizing my secret time with Papa, I am fulfilling His commandment to Jeremiah: *thus speaketh the Lord God of Israel, saying, write thee all the words that I have spoken unto thee in a book (Jeremiah 30:2).* I want to put it in writing lest it vanish like a vapor and be lost forever. If we invest in journalizing these precious times, not on loose pages that might be lost, but in a book, it will be a legacy for future generations.

As William Wordsworth wrote: "fill your pages with the breathings of your heart."[23]

---

[23] William Wordsworth, A quote from a Letter to His Wife, April 29, 1812.

CHAPTER EIGHT

HIDDEN MANNA

He that hath an ear, let him hear what the Spirit saith unto the
churches; To him that overcometh will I give to eat of the hidden
manna (Revelation 2:17).

During Israel's wandering in the wilderness, God faithfully fed them manna to sustain their bodies. Today God is still feeding His people manna, but this manna will sustain their souls.

Throughout their forty years of wandering they worshipped God in a portable house of gold, called the Tabernacle. The blueprint of the Tabernacle was given to Moses on the mount at which time he also received the Decalogue, the two tablets of stone engraved with the Ten Commandments. I am sure we have all seen a statue of Moses holding forth the Ten Commandments. Yet how often have we seen Moses also holding forth the blueprint of the Tabernacle? We do the Word an injustice by elevating the importance of one and minimizing the other. One speaks of God's holiness, truth and righteousness while the other speaks of His mercy and peace towards sinful mankind. What an awesome picture this is of God's holiness and God's mercy. What an inspiring, clear-cut portrayal of

God's plan of salvation is illustrated in this blueprint, a foreshadow of the redemption of Calvary!

Here we have, on the one hand, the Decalogue showing His holiness and His standards, which God knew we couldn't live up to it because of our fallen nature: *for all have sinned, and come short of the glory of God (1 John 3: 4); whosoever committeth sin transgresseth also the law: for sin is the transgression of the law (Romans 3: 23).* And on the other hand we have the blueprint of His plan of salvation that would show us the only way possible for sinful man to draw near a holy God. Because of His love and mercy toward fallen man He still wanted to have fellowship with us. That blueprint of His plan of salvation was the layout of the Tabernacle. *And there I will meet with thee, and I will commune with thee from above the mercy seat, from between the two cherubims which are upon the ark of the testimony (Exodus 25:22).* The Tablets of the Decalogue were placed inside the Ark of the Covenant and covered by a lid, which was the mercy seat, where two cherubim stretched forth their wings to touch each other. *Mercy and truth are met together; righteousness and peace have kissed each other (Psalm 85:10).* Surely this picture beautifully portrays this scripture. It is important to interject another look at the Tabernacle here, as we search for a more intimate relationship with God, because it is only on the fulfillment of this shadowy blueprint that we have a basis to draw near to God.

There were two other objects placed in the Ark. *Which had the golden censer, and the ark of the covenant overlaid round about with gold, wherein was the golden pot that had manna, and Aaron's rod that budded, and the tables of the covenant (Hebrews 9: 4).* There was Aaron's rod that miraculously budded overnight, which speaks to us of the resurrection, and a pot of manna to remind Israel of God's provision. *And Moses said unto Aaron, Take a pot, and put an omer full of manna therein, and lay it up before the Lord, to be kept for your generations (Exodus 16: 33).* This 'hidden" pot of manna in the Ark is the topic of this chapter and the reason I call the words which I journal "Hidden Manna."

The Tabernacle was divided into three sections. An Outer Court where the blood was shed on the Brazen Altar, and where the priests would cleanse themselves at the Brazen Laver before entering the Holy Place to minister unto God. The Golden Candlestick, the Golden Table of Shrewbread and the Golden Altar of Incense were all placed in the Holy Place. Lastly but no means the least was the most reverent place of all, the Holy of Holies, where the only light was the Shekinah glory of God. This is where God promised to meet with Moses from above the mercy seat that covered the Ark of the Covenant. This place of communion is a place one must come alone to meet with God. The Holy of Holies is the only place that hidden manna is to be found. To reach this place of communion we must press through in humble boldness, gratitude and holiness (see chapter on "Pressing on into His Presence").

Dear Child,

Hidden manna is only fed to those who will press into My presence. Hidden manna is not fed in the Outer Court. It is only fed to overcomers who seek Me with all their hearts. It is for those who come alone for a time of fellowship and intimacy with Me! Only this manna can refresh and strengthen you that you might have the power to be an overcomer.

Thus saith Papa.

So as we invest the time to press through and draw near He will feed us hidden manna.

Jesus refers to this as spiritual food for the overcomers in Revelation 2:17: *He that hath an ear, let him hear what the Spirit saith unto the churches; To him that overcometh will I give to eat of the hidden manna, and will give him a white stone, and in the stone a new name written, which no man knoweth saving he that receiveth it.* The Living Bible translates 'hidden manna' as 'secret nourishment from heaven'.

Matthew Henry's commentary quotes on this verse is interesting: "the hidden manna, the influences and spirit of Christ in communion with him, coming down from heaven into the soul, from time to time, for its support, to let it taste something how saints and angels live in heaven. This hidden from the rest of the world - a stranger intermeddles not with this joy: and it is laid up in Christ, the ark of the covenant, in the Holy of Holies."[24]

---

[24] Matthew Henry, *op. cit.,* Volume 6, p.1128.

My Prayer:

Dear Father,
Thank you for your Word and for ears to hear it. Thank you
for the Holy Spirit to teach it, and your grace available to
live it. Help me daily as I read your Word, to hide it deep in
my heart, lest the enemy comes and steals it away. Help me
daily to faithfully spend my time with you that I might have
deep roots through my secret history alone with you. I know
it's only with these deep roots, the enemy cannot pull up and
steal the word from my heart. It's buried deep in the soil of
my heart and hidden! With your help, Lord, it will with
patience bear good fruit that has been brought to perfection.
In His loving Name, Amen!

His answer:

Dear Child,
That is the hidden manna of your heart! Your secret history
is that path I walk with you that nobody else knows of, that
secret history is time spent with the One who knows you the
best and loves you the most. Only I know all the motivation
of your heart and thoughts, only you and I know your
innermost being. Your history and communications with
Me, will be the path we can share, as I alone can deal with
those motivations that are not of My Spirit, and daily
transform you into My likeness as we spend time together.
Thus saith Papa.

Just as the hidden manna was concealed in the Ark of the Covenant in the Holy of Holies, even so my hidden manna is concealed
in my heart, the Holy of Holies of my temple where God by His

grace now dwells. As the Psalmist wrote: *"thy word have I hid in mine heart, that I might not sin against thee" (Psalm 119:11).*

As previously mentioned, when the Lord speaks to our hearts He speaks to us individually in a language we will understand. He will serve us manna that we will be able to digest. He speaks to me through my love and study of the Tabernacle or through my love of gardening. He uses these two passions as windows to my soul, which causes His words to be applicable to my life. As we study the gospels we see how Jesus taught His disciples spiritual truths through parables from their culture and lifestyles. For example we see Him teaching them in the language of farming or fishing. This they could grasp as He painted pictures of spiritual truths in a language they understood. As you attentively listen for that still, small voice, you will hear Him in a language you can understand, as you hungrily seek Him, He will fill your mouth with manna you can digest.

> *Ask, and it shall be given you; seek, and ye shall find; knock, and it shall be opened unto you: For every one that asketh receiveth; and he that seeketh findeth; and to him that knocketh it shall be opened. Or what man is there of you, whom if his son ask bread, will he give him a stone? Or if he ask a fish, will he give him a serpent? If ye then, being evil, know how to give good gifts unto your children, how much more shall your Father which is in heaven give good things to them that ask him? (Matthew 7: 7-11).*

We could use the metaphor of the Holy Spirit as a musician; the music is the truth of the Word; and the instruments are individual believers. A musician plays three different instruments, e.g.: piano, organ and violin. The three instruments possess their own unique sound. Therefore each performance will be a different work of art. Even though the musician is the same and the music is the same, each instrument will provide its own unique flavor, color and feel.

In the four gospels each different evangelist gives us a picture of the Lord in four different dimensions. How this enriches our understanding of Him. Far from clouding our view of God's Word, it enhances and interprets it all the more wonderfully. So it will be as you journalize your hidden manna, it will be the same Holy Spirit, the same truth, but written in a different language than mine.

Within the body we have those who are spiritually anorexic because they refuse to open their mouths and eat the manna. Unlike the psalmist who wrote: *I opened my mouth, and panted: for I longed for thy commandments (Psalm 119:131)*. We must be like baby birds who sit with their mouths wide open ready to eat whatever their mothers place in their mouths.

> *But thou, son of man, hear what I say unto thee; Be not thou rebellious like that rebellious house: open thy mouth, and eat that I give thee. And when I looked, behold, a hand was sent unto me; and, lo, a roll of a book was therein (Ezekiel 2:8-10).*

According to Matthew Henry's Commentary "to eat" in the verse above means "admit this revelation into thy understanding, take it, take the meaning of it, understand it aright, admit it into thy heart, apply and be affected with it."[25]

And we have those that suffer from spiritual bulimia because they throw up that which they have swallowed and empty their stomach instead of filling it.

Moreover he said unto me, Son of man, eat that thou findest; eat this roll, and go speak unto the house of Israel. And he said unto me, Son of man, cause thy belly to eat, and fill thy stomach with this roll that I give thee. Then did I eat it; and it was in my mouth as honey for sweetness (Ezekiel 3:1-3).

Matthew Henry also states that "cause thy belly to eat and fill thy stomach with it" means "do not eat it and bring it up again as that which is nauseous but eat it and retain it as that which is nourishing to the stomach."[26]

Dear Child,
Take heed and walk the words I feed you, only then will that manna remain fresh, or else it will become a stench! To stay fresh and stay alive you must digest it that it will become part of every cell of your being. Remember the manna which I feed you will only remain fresh to feed others, as you take it in, digest it, hide it in your heart and live it.
It will only profit you as you eat it! It will only profit others as you live it!
Just as Israel ate of the manna which I provided, only that which they ate did not deteriorate and begin to stink. Hypocrisy is a stench! Words but no walk! Only that which you walk will give life to others! The rest is dead works.
Thus saith Papa.

Beware ye of the leaven of the Pharisees, which is hypocrisy (Luke 12:1).

---

[25] Matthew Henry, *op. cit.,* Volume 4, p. 762.
[26] Matthew Henry, *op. cit.,* Volume 4, p. 763.

The manna that Israel picked had to be gathered early in the morning before the heat of the day melted it. Likewise we also need to find our manna early in the day before the heat of trials or testings cross our path. As I was reflecting on this I prayed:

Father,
It is so good to spend this time alone with You in the early morning at my rose garden, before the busyness and hecticness of the day begins. Surely in the freshness of the day, I receive fresh manna from your hand, to sustain me through the heat of the day. Testings that will try my faith. Choices that will test the authenticity of my faith. Distractions that will absorb me, and pull me away from my faith and my walk.

He replied:

Dear Child,
Manna from My hand is always fresh, but how can it sustain you through the day if you don't eat or partake of it until later in the day? Would you start the day without breakfast? Nourish your soul early and drink of Me before the heat of the day drains you of spiritual energy. Be full of Me early to sustain you through the day, no matter what the day may bring.
Thus saith Papa.

When the Israelites found the miraculous food lying on the ground, *"they said one to another, It is manna: for they wist not what it was. And Moses said unto them, this is the bread which the Lord hath given you to eat (Exodus 16:15).* The word 'manna' means 'what is it?' Likewise as we look at the Word, we ask: 'what is it?' And question: 'what does this mean?' The natural man does not know, only through spiritual eyes can we understand the spirit of the Word. The natural man can only see the cold letter of the Word. As I spend time alone with the Lord, He takes the husk off the heavenly corn, that I might be able to digest the manna and appropriate it to my life. He feeds me nourishment for my soul. The natural man only feeds on the dry husk, the membranous outer covering, which is the dry cold letter of the Word. *And had rained down manna upon them to eat, and had given them of the corn of heaven (Psalm 78:24).* This corn of heaven is to satisfy the hunger of the soul. If we only hunger after knowledge we will be merely feeding on the barren husks of the corn, which contain no spiritual life because the husk has no seeds of life. God programmed seed to produce life, and just as husks cannot produce life, even so the cold letter of the Word cannot produce spiritual life.

As I was meditating on the experience of the two who encountered the risen Lord on the road to Emmaus (Luke 24:13-31), I saw footprints from their journey that I could follow in my fellowship with the Lord.

1. They not only invited Him to stay with them, they compelled Him to stay.

   He will also sup with us if we open the door and invite Him to fellowship with us.

2. As Jesus blessed and broke the bread, their eyes were opened and they knew Him.

   He will also break manna for us and strip the heavenly corn of its husks. Only then will our spiritual eyes be opened and we will see Him in the Word.

3. Their hearts burned within them as He talked with them and opened the Scriptures to them.

   As we attentively listen for His voice during our quiet time alone, there will be a witness in our spirits as our hearts burn within us, while He talks to us and opens the Scriptures to us.

As I continued my pilgrim journey in their indelible footprints, I prayed this prayer:

Dear Father,
As I study with the help and guidance of the Holy Spirit, rightly dividing the Word, may I learn and not only know the Scriptures, but also the spiritual power of those Scriptures. May they lead me to know and see Your heart! I cry as the gospel writer wrote in John 12:21 "I would see Jesus" for truly, Lord, they speak of You. Do those words have any power if I don't see Jesus in them?

He told me:

Dear Child,
If you don't see Me, you don't see the Word with spiritual eyes, for am I not the Word? They speak of Me for I am the Word. If you don't see Me in the Word, you don't see the Truth, for I am the Truth. If you don't see Me in the Word, you don't see the Way, for I am the Way.

I am Alpha and Omega, the beginning and the end. There is no word outside of that, I am A to Z. You will find Me in the Word if you search for Me with all your heart. If you search just for knowledge you will not find Me. You must search for Me.
I am your inspiration.
I am your doctrine for life.
I am your teacher.
I am your righteousness.
Search for ME!
Thus saith Papa.

In 2 Kings 3:16-27, there is a record of God's miraculous deliverance of Israel. The only thing God required of them was to dig ditches, and He would do the rest. We must do the mundane things and then God will do the miraculous! They did the digging and God did the filling. What a lesson we can learn from this story. As we faithfully dig into the Word, He will fill the ditches with living water.

Behold, thou desirest truth in the inward parts: and in the hidden part thou shalt make me to know wisdom (Psalm 51:6).

As we develop a secret history with God, He will cause us to know the truth, the wisdom and power of His Word in our hidden root structure, where our character is formed while we are being conformed to His Image. While reading over my past journals of hidden manna, I realized how God was using this time to conform me, because my journalizing was more about who I was becoming rather than directions of what I should be doing (see chapter "Changed from glory to glory"). We must understand that it is not about deep knowledge, but rather it is all about a deep relationship with our Heavenly Father, who has promised, *"I will give you the treasures of darkness and riches hidden in secret places, so that you may know that it is I, the Lord, the God of Israel, who call you by your name" (Isaiah 45:3).* I consider these riches as my hidden manna that Papa drops into the deep recesses of my heart to develop my relationship with Him, and to build my faith and confidence in that relationship.

I want to encourage you to ask the Lord for "your daily bread." Remember the manna had to be picked not only early but also daily. After attentively waiting on Him in silence, pick up your pen and start writing in faith the precious words He is speaking to you. You will, in fact, be recording your spiritual history and walk with God. What a legacy to leave your children and loved ones. We all keep albums of photos to record our biological history, so why not keep a record of our spiritual history. Our journals will be a silent witness of our footprints of faith that will challenge and deepen the spiritual journey of those who follows us.

> *Dear Child,*
> *As you write these words you are making inerasable footprints for others to follow, to show them the way to where I have taken you, that where I am you may also be, followed by your loved ones and those whose lives you have touched.*

These footprints will be a legacy of gold tried by fire, the legacy of your faith walk with Me daily. These will be bearing fruit even after you are with Me.
Thus saith Papa.

Be ye followers of me, even as I also am of Christ (1 Corinthians 11:1).

CHAPTER NINE

PRESSING ON INTO HIS PRESENCE

*I press toward the mark for the prize of the high calling
of God in Christ Jesus (Philippians 3:14).*

In the Outer Court we have a personal relationship with the Father because of the blood on the Brazen Altar, where sacrificial lambs were slain.

In the Holy Place, which is a type of the church, we have a corporate relationship. It was where the priests would break bread together at the Golden Table of Shewbread, as they walked in the light of the Golden Candlestick to have fellowship one with another.

If we walk in the light, as he is in the light, we have fellowship one with another (1 John 1:7).

But only as we press on into the Holy of Holies alone can we have an intimate relationship with the Father. Intimacy is something shared by only two – you and God.

In the Outer Court we seek His hand for what He has done for us, but in the Holy of Holies we seek His face that we might know who He is.

- In the Outer Court we minister for Him, but in the Holiest Place we minister to Him.

- In the Outer Court we are doing, but in the Holiest Place we are becoming.

- In the Outer Court I am His servant, but in the Holiest Place I am His child.

We cannot minister to Him from afar we must draw near. Who can draw near? David received the answer: *Lord, who shall abide in thy tabernacle? who shall dwell in thy holy hill? He that walketh uprightly, and worketh righteousness, and speaketh the truth in his heart (Psalm 15:1-2).*

> *But the priests the Levites, the sons of Zadok, that kept the charge of my sanctuary when the children of Israel went astray from me, they shall come near to me to minister unto me, and they shall stand before me to offer unto me the fat and the blood, saith the Lord God (Ezekiel 44:15).*

Watchman Nee says: "one basic condition to all that can truly be called ministry to the Lord is that we draw near to Him. He desires our worship; yet how hard we find it to drag ourselves into His presence! We shrink from the solitude, and even when we do detach ourselves physically from outside things, we find our thoughts wandering back to them."[27]

Many of us can enjoy working among people in the Outer Court, but how many give time to draw near to God in the Holy Place? To come into His presence and wait upon Him demands all the determination we possess, and might even mean that we may have to be vehement with ourselves. But let me be very frank with you, it is impossible to stand afar off and yet minister to Him. You cannot serve God from a distance. In the Outer Court, quite rightly you

---

[27] Watchman Nee, *op. cit.,* Devotion April 18.

approach people, but in the Holy Place you approach the Lord. Come nearer. It is your privilege.

There once hung a veil separating us from God's presence, but when Jesus cried out "It is finished," that veil was rent supernaturally from the top to the bottom. His sacrificial death paid the price that we may once again come into His presence. When Moses came down from the Mount where he had communed with God, he wore a veil over his face to hide the glory. But Jesus took away the veil that we might behold His glory! His broken body is our spiritual access: *by a new and living way, which he hath consecrated for us, through the veil, that is to say, his flesh (Hebrews 10:20).* In the Old Testament the priest would offer his prayer at the Golden Altar of Incense, where the prayer would seep through the veil into God's presence. Through the New Covenant, believers still offer their prayer through a veil, but that veil is the broken body of The Lord Jesus, that is to say we offer prayer in His Name and through His Name.

Verily, verily, I say unto you, Whatsoever ye shall ask the Father in my name, he will give it you. Hitherto have ye asked nothing in my name: ask, and ye shall receive, that your joy may be full (John 16:23-24).

In the Old Testament God dwelt in the Holiest of Holies in the Tabernacle. *And let them make me a sanctuary; that I may dwell among them (Exodus 25:8).*

In the Gospels He dwelt in the Lord Jesus. *For in Him dwelleth all the fullness of the Godhead bodily (Colossians 2:9).*

In the current church age He dwells in believers. *What? Know ye not that your body is the temple of the Holy Ghost which is in you, which ye have of God, and ye are not your own? (1 Corinthians 6: 19).* Before we turn to Christ there is still a veil over our hearts that blinds us from the glory of the truth. As we surrender our lives to Him, the veil is taken away, or should I say that the flesh of our old man is torn away. Surely this is spiritual circumcision.

> *But he is a Jew, which is one inwardly; and circumcision is that of the heart, in the spirit, and not in the letter (Romans 2:29); in whom also ye are circumcised with the circumcision made without hands, in putting off the body of the sins of the flesh by the circumcision of Christ (Colossians 2:11).*

At the moment of this spiritual circumcision God comes to dwell in the heart of the believer, because our hearts are now the Holiest of Holies. So our lives are not acceptable to God because of what we do outwardly, even denying the flesh, without an inner rendering of the heart. Then God works through us from inwardly, that our lives might outwardly bring glory to His name. If we only rent the outward we are putting on a self-made garment. Our garment must be one of His righteousness worked out through a rent heart where He dwells.

If we were going on a job interview we would dress appropriately, or if we had an audience with the Queen of England it would be mandatory, as a woman, to include a hat and white gloves in my attire. However unlike other appointments with people, we don't prepare our appearance to approach God but rather we prepare our hearts. *For the Lord seeth not as man seeth; for man looketh on the outward appearance, but the Lord looketh on the heart (1 Samuel 16:7).* We don't wear certain attire but rather we clothe our hearts with certain attitudes. As we approach the throne we clothe our hearts in an attitude of:

1. Gratitude
2. Humility
3. Holiness in reverent fear

We draw near to praise Him clothed in gratitude with thanksgiving. We draw near to fellowship and grow in His presence clothed with a contrite and humble heart. We draw near to worship Him clothed in holiness.

1. Gratitude

Enter into his gates with thanksgiving, and into his courts with praise: be thankful unto him, and bless his name (Psalm 100:4).

An attitude of praise is the result of a thankful heart. Praise and thanksgiving are like Siamese twins, they are inseparable. Without thanksgiving we haven't even entered the gate into His presence. Yet so often we try to offer praise in His court, and yet we find ourselves still on the outside. This is a lesson we can learn from the specific placement of each of the tribes of Israel around the Tabernacle. Outside the only entrance into the Outer Court, God chose to place the tribe of Judah, whose name means 'praise', that we might understand that those who praise Him are closest to His presence. But even those with a heart to praise Him must also have a heart of gratitude, or they cannot come into His presence. The only way into His presence is through the Gate of Thanksgiving (Psalm 100:4). So often we come to church with a heavy heart because of circumstances. But if only we would spend a few moments reflecting and counting our blessings, as the Word tells us *"bless the Lord oh my soul, and forget not all his benefits" (Psalm 103:2);* it would give us an appreciative, thankful heart, and our attitude would change preparing us to enter the gate and into His courts with praise. He has promised us *"the garment of praise for the spirit of heaviness" (Isaiah 61:3).* Please note that I did not say our circumstances would necessarily change, I said our attitude to the circumstances would change! We will no longer be under the circumstances because our sacrifice of praise will raise us above those circumstances, and we will find ourselves spiritually seated in Heavenly places in Christ Jesus. *And hath raised us up together, and made us sit together in heavenly places in Christ Jesus (Ephesians 2:6).* Then in His timing we will see victory because He can work with those who praise Him.

What has eaten away at this attitude of gratitude? Could it be a lack of appreciation, discontentment or complaining? A grateful heart is a soft, pliable heart in the loving hands of the Master Potter. But hearts become cold and hardened when we murmur and complain. Hearts become distant and lukewarm when appreciating all the Lord has done for us. Hearts exchang for stress when we become discontented. Where there is true worship there is no complaining. The heart of a true worshipper is a heart of gratitude, humility and holiness.

> *Then Job arose, and rent his mantle, and shaved his head, and fell down upon the ground, and worshipped, And said, Naked came I out of my mother's womb, and naked shall I return thither: the Lord gave, and the Lord hath taken away; blessed be the name of the Lord. In all this Job sinned not, nor charged God foolishly (Job 1:20-22).*

> *And when the people complained, it displeased the Lord: and the Lord heard it; and his anger was kindled; and the fire of the Lord burnt among them, and consumed them that were in the uttermost parts of the camp (Numbers 11:1).*

Since we are only made happy by what we appreciate, why do we wonder what happened to our joy when we begin to take the blessings in our lives for granted. Therefore if we want more joy in our lives we need to appreciate what the Lord has provided for us even more. When we cry unto the Lord, *"restore unto me the joy of thy salvation" (Psalm 51:12);* we are really crying out for a grateful heart! A complaining heart soon becomes a heart drowning in self-pity that will quench your joy. The fruit of thankfulness is joy and joy results in spiritual strength. *"...neither be ye sorry; for the joy of the Lord is your strength" (Nehemiah 8:10).*

We bless and please the Lord when we are thankful: *I will praise the name of God with a song, and will magnify him with thanksgiving. This also shall please the Lord better than an ox or bullock that hath horns and hoofs (Psalm 69:30).*

If you want to come into His presence, come with thanksgiving: *O come, let us sing unto the Lord: let us make a joyful noise to the rock of our salvation. Let us come before his presence with thanksgiving, and make a joyful noise unto him with psalms (Psalm 95:1-2).*

> *Dear Child,*
> *Having a thankful heart is living the abundant life!*
> *Having a thankful heart is a life full of joy!*
> *Having a thankful heart is a life that can be molded to My will!*
> *Having a thankful heart is the life of a true worshipper!*
> *Thus saith Papa.*

Yes, it is hard when we are burdened and we just don't feel like praising God, but isn't that what a sacrifice of praise is all about? Something that is costing you! What is the cost? An act of our will to choose to praise Him, even when we do not understand the 'whys?' We are actually confirming our faith with that praise: "God, I don't know the future but I believe that you hold my future and I trust you with the outcome." We call that faith and without faith it is impossible to please Him. *By him therefore let us offer the sacrifice of praise to God continually, that is, the fruit of our lips giving thanks to his name (Hebrews 13:15).* May we all grow to the stature of the faith of Job. *Though he slay me, yet will I trust in him (Job 13:15).*

Happiness is passive; it depends on outside sources, in other words it depends on good happenings. Therefore when there are adverse circumstances we are not happy. Joy on the other hand is active and is from within. What has robbed us of our joy especially as Christians? May I suggest a lack of gratitude? Does the world see us as joy-killers? Joy is not the absence of turmoil and hard times from without, but rather from the delight of God's presence from within. Do you take your blessings for granted or with gratitude?

Many Americans express dissatisfaction with life, despite the fact that we have more of the world's good things than any other country. The richest country in the world is inhabited by the highest percentage of depressed and unhappy people. The human emotional apparatus is constructed so as to disregard that which is taken for granted. The best immune system booster is a shot of super joy. Our emotions are related to the functioning of our immune system. A modern day psychology book, *The Law of Life*, states "We are not made happy by what we acquire but by what we appreciate." A survey in the book revealed that we usually take for granted 80% of the blessings in our lives, therefore we are only 20% as happy as we could be! Consequently the degree to which we are thankful determines our happiness; the degree to which we rejoice in the Lord determines our spiritual strength.

How often have you heard and even said to yourself, "if only I had so and so? Or if only I could do so and so? Then I would be happy!" All the things we think we absolutely must have in order to be happy are only indications that we are controlled from without rather than from within. It is an endless trap that we can never escape as long as we think that ownership of something is going to fill the void. When will we ever be satisfied with enough 'stuff'? The Bible warns us that we will never be satisfied: *hell and destruction are never full; so the eyes of man are never satisfied (Proverbs 27:20).*

'Stuff' is there to serve you rather than make you a servant. Have you ever found that after only a few months of ownership of a new car, new house or new clothes etc; they only give us a small portion of the pleasure that we received when we first obtained them as blessings. Why? Because we no longer appreciate the blessings as much as we did when we first received them!

This same principle could be also applied to our marriages and even our relationship with God. When we start to take our partners for granted, we become bored with each other, and wonder whatever happened to that spark of joy? A spirit of thanklessness will always cause boredom to set in. If we begin to take our great salvation for granted, we may even find ourselves becoming bored with God and life will soon disintegrate. Neurotics focus on what he lacks rather than on what he possesses. If we fail to see God's blessings, and concentrate on lack, we lose our joy, and it is replaced with depression and heaviness. We become spiritually bored and find we cannot praise the Lord. When we focus on God's abundant mercy we are uplifted. Some complain that God put thorns on roses while others praise God that He put roses on thorns!

Discard the scarcity mentality by giving thanks for everything. Truly appreciate the miracle of who you are. The fact that you are alive, you have eyes to see, ears to hear, hands to touch, feet to walk, imagination that you can dream! Make an effort to focus on what you have, rather than on what you are missing. Focus on being thankful for all you do have. You have water to quench your thirst, the sun that warms you, the air you breathe and everything good and perfect thing which is a gift from God.

Every good gift and every perfect gift is from above, and cometh down from the Father of lights (James 1:17).

As you practice being thankful, expand the list of things that you are thankful for: e.g. family, friends, clothes, food, etc. You will be using your thoughts to dwell on appreciation of your abundance. We all need a revaluation of life. Super joy and increased appreciation, even amazement, for the smallest details of life go hand in hand. Try to discover some of the amazement of your childhood.

Complaining is the twin of self-pity. Self-pity is the most crippling disease known to man. People have conquered diseases such as paralysis, blindness and leprosy and lived happy, useful lives, but not until they first conquered self-pity. If we wait for everything we want accomplished to be completed before we celebrate, we will miss the party of life! Most symphonic works end with a major chord, the 'da, da' that gives us a sense of completion and finality. "As soon as the children are finished with college and I have vested interest in my retirement plan, we're going to start to live a little ourselves" said one man. This 'da, da' approach to life restricts our joy as we await a major chord that will never come. The symphony of life is forever an unfinished symphony written primarily in minor chords, and you will not enjoy the entire concert, if you live in expectation of a final signal note to begin your joy.

This is the day which the Lord hath made; we will rejoice and be glad in it (Psalm 118:24).

Dear Child,

If you appreciated all My blessings in your life, your heart would overflow with joy! Giving thanks causes you to be reminded of what you are thankful for and this gives you a fresh appreciation. If you are thankful for My blessings, you will enjoy them, if you take them for granted they will not give you joy, for they will be put on the shelf for another day like a discarded gift. Enjoy life, it's My greatest gift, when you enjoy life you have a thankful heart, and a thankful heart is pleasing in My sight.

Thus saith Papa.

Let your conversation be without covetousness; and be content with such things as ye have: for he hath said, I will never leave thee, nor forsake thee (Hebrews 13:5).

Truly one of the keys of true contentment is a sense of inward sufficiency, which only comes from our relationship to our Heavenly Papa. With appreciation and thankfulness for His provision let us be content. Let us be satisfied with ENOUGH!

➢ Lucifer was the highest of the angels in heaven yet not content!
➢ Adam was in paradise yet not content!
➢ Angels were in heaven yet not content!
➢ Haman had a great court position yet not content!
➢ Ahab was on a throne yet not content!

> *Dear Child,*
> *A thankful heart is an appreciative heart, and an appreciative heart is a soft heart, which I can work with and mold, but an ungrateful heart becomes hard and cold. With appreciation comes contentment. Godliness and contentment are great gain. So fulfill My will for you today, be thankful and you will be contented.*
> *Thus saith Papa.*

But godliness with contentment is great gain. For we brought nothing into this world, and it is certain we can carry nothing out. And having food and raiment let us be therewith content (1 Timothy 6:6-8).

I want to give us some food for thought with a list of things which money can and cannot buy. Money will buy:

- A bed BUT not sleep
- Books BUT not brains
- Food BUT not an appetite
- Finery BUT not beauty
- A house BUT not a home
- Medicine BUT not health
- Luxuries BUT not culture

- Amusement BUT not happiness
- A crucifix BUT not a savior
- A church pew BUT not heaven.

For I have learned, in whatsoever state I am, therewith to be content (Philippians 4:11).

Don't try to keep up with the 'Jones'! Rather be content. Contentment comes not so much from great wealth but from few wants! Why does God continually remind us to be thankful?

- A thankful heart is full of praise, which ushers us into His presence.
- A thankful heart blesses the Father's heart.
- A thankful heart is a soft, pliable heart that God can mold to His image.
- A thankful heart is a joyous heart that strengthens us spiritually.
- A thankful heart remembers His faithfulness in the past thereby feeding our faith to trust Him for our future.
- A thankful heart will be a good steward of blessings.

Dear Child,

Entering My presence with thanksgiving will build the faith you need to present your requests before Me, for without faith it is impossible to please Me! Without thanksgiving you will not have that ever increasing faith to believe that I am a rewarder of those who diligently seek Me! Because thanksgiving brings to remembrance My faithfulness in the past and feeds your faith. But ingratitude produces a complaining heart drowned in self-pity, which will quench your faith. An unthankful heart will be excluded from My presence. In My presence is joy unspeakable and full of

glory, a place you can only enter through the gate of thanks-
giving! Child, be thankful!
Thus saith Papa, My Jehovah Jireh.

In everything give thanks: for this is the will of God in Christ Jesus
concerning you. Quench not the Spirit (1 Thessalonians 5:18-19).

Have the moths of discontentment, complaining and lack of appreciation eaten away holes in your garment of praise, leaving it thread bare, and robbing your life of joy? Without heartfelt appreciation and thankfulness we are only offering God an empty lip service!

2. Humility

As we prepare our hearts to draw near to fellowship and grow in His presence let us be aware that the key to His presence is humility.

For thus saith the high and lofty One that inhabiteth eternity, whose name is
Holy; I dwell in the high and holy place, with him also that is of a contrite and
humble spirit, to revive the spirit of the humble, and to revive the heart of the
contrite ones (Isaiah 57:15).

We are exhorted to come boldly to the throne, but boldness without humility is only arrogance.

Dear Child,
Your boldness comes from confidence of your relationship
with Me as we spend time together; your boldness comes
from respecting the holiness of My presence; your boldness
comes from not defiling My temple; your boldness comes
from obeying My word at the Laver.

Otherwise it is not holy boldness but only carnal assumption. Boldness without humility is only arrogance.
Thus saith Papa.

Our bold confidence should not be portrayed, as an arrogance that is demanding of its rights, but rather as humility that is ever grateful of our privileges as a child of God. We dare not walk in self-confidence for the self-life must be crucified. But rather we must walk in the sanctified self-confidence: *I can do all things through Christ which strengtheneth me (Philippians 4:13).* Or as the Amplified Bible puts it, *I have strength for all things in Christ Who empowers me - I am ready for anything and equal to anything through Him Who infuses inner strength into me, that is I am self-sufficient in Christ's sufficiency.*

We must allow God to nullify our self-sufficiency. When we humbly confess before Him that we can do nothing in our own strength, then Christ will be able to manifest His power upon us. That which passes through the death of the cross and rises up again in newness life is of God, and being so, will count mightily for Him. We must root our self-sufficiency in Christ's sufficiency, that our confidence will be in our relationship to Him and not in ourselves.

Not that we are sufficient of ourselves to think any thing as of ourselves; but our sufficiency is of God (2 Corinthians 3:5).

I prayed:

Dear Father

Protect me from myself, that is my own self- confidence, for in the day of trial it will fail me. Protect me with a confidence that only comes from my total trust and dependence on You, and my relationship to You, because of Your mercy and grace paid for by the precious blood of the spotless Lamb of God.

Help me in my daily walk, that I will not deny Your presence in my life by my actions and words before the world.

Help me realize more and more that time spent with You is not a nonproductive activity but my very life line to the power to live for You!

He replied:

Dear Child,

Draw near more and more, that I may teach you, that I may feed you manna from heaven and the water that will give you eternal life, and will refresh you daily during your pilgrim walk.

It is easy not to deny Me while in My presence in the Holy Place, the test is when you leave to walk in the Outer Court, where you mix with the world. It was before sinners that Peter denied Me! Walk in the Outer Court in the strength which I will impart to you in the Holy Place, not in your own strength and self-confidence. Self will fail you. For self must die. Many worship Me in church but the test comes when they leave My house! It is not how high you jump before Me, but how straight you walk in the Outer Court. Many swear their love for Me in My presence, but when the

test comes in the Outer Court, they deny Me by their actions
and words!
Lean on Me and allow self to die. That I might rule and
guide you in your walk.
Have confidence in who 'I AM'.
Thus saith Papa.

Obviously the self-righteous Pharisee of Luke 18 did not recognize his inadequacy, but the publican humbly cried on the mercy of God. Which one pressed through to His presence and left justified? *I tell you, this man went down to his house justified rather than the other: for every one that exalteth himself shall be abased; and he that humbleth himself shall be exalted (Luke 18:14).* Indeed the humble publican pressed through and was justified!

Through the floor of the tabernacle God gives us a picture lesson in humility. The floor was only the dust of the desert. *The dust that is in the floor of the tabernacle (Numbers 5:17).* And even when the priest would step into the beautiful Holy Place with walls of gold, he had to walk on a floor that was still only dust. As the Word tells us: *for dust thou art, and unto dust shalt thou return (Genesis 3:19).* Even when we press through to step into His Presence we are reminded from this lesson that we are still only dust, lest we become elevated by being in His presence, for God will not share His Glory! *I am the Lord: that is my name: and my glory will I not give to another (Isaiah 42:8).* Even in the Holiest of Holies, where the shekinah glory of God dwelt, the floor was still only dust. May we be ever reminded from the floor of dust in the tabernacle to walk humbly before Him: *that no flesh should glory in his presence! (1 Corinthians 12:9).*

Yes, we are redeemed but only redeemed dust until that day when: *who shall change our vile body, that it may be fashioned like unto his glorious body (Philippians 3:21).* On the day of our glorification we shall no longer walk on dust, but indeed in the tabernacle whose streets are gold: *and the twelve gates were twelve pearls: every several gate was of one pearl: and the street of the city was pure gold, as it were transparent glass (Revelation 21: 21).*

The name ADAM signifies earth, red earth. God gave Adam his name. Adam named all other creatures but not his own, lest he should assume some glorious pompous title, but God gave him a name to remind him of the meanness of his origin. Those have little reason to be proud who are so akin to dust. But there is more to us than dust. *And the Lord God formed man of the dust of the ground, and breathed into his nostrils the breath of life; and man became a living soul (Genesis 2:7).* Here Ken Gire's viewpoint is interesting:

> We have a mingling of blood within us from a lineage that is both human and divine. Within us the dust of the earth and the breath of heaven are joined in a mysterious union that only death can separate. But that relationship is often a strained one, for while the body is fitted for a terrestrial environment - with lungs to breathe air, teeth to chew food and feet to walk on dirt- the spirit is extraterrestrial, fitted for heaven. It breathes other air, eats other food and walks on other terrain.[28]

---

[28] Ken Gire, *op. cit.,* p. 48.

God reminded me:

Dear Child,
The flesh cannot conceive anything that is of the spirit.
Humility is a fruit of the Spirit, so do not try to manufac-
ture a humility that you can be proud of. You can only walk
humbly before Me as you walk in the spirit. Remember the
dust! Only the heart and trial of your faith are gold!
Thus saith Papa.

Let it be the hidden man of the heart, in that which is not corruptible, even the
ornament of a meek and quiet spirit, which is in the sight of God of great price
(1 Peter 3:4).

Even though the body is dust, the inner man where God dwells by His Spirit is a golden sanctuary. In the Old Testament, God dwelt in the Holy of Holies where not only the ark and mercy seat were pure gold but even the walls. In the New Testament age God now dwells in another Holy of Holies, the heart of the believer. A good person is said to have a 'heart of gold'. The origin of this phrase is from the concept of God indwelling the heart of a believer.

And the Lord God said unto the serpent, Because thou hast done this, thou art
cursed above all cattle, and above every beast of the field; upon thy belly shalt
thou go, and dust shalt thou eat all the days of thy life (Genesis 3: 14).

By feeding the lusts of the flesh, which is only dust, we are giving the serpent more to feed on and more to hold over us. But when we humble ourselves and deny the lusts of the flesh, they will die and the serpent will have nothing in our lives to feed on or hold over us.

Humility is your protection against deception. We are warned in Proverbs that *"bread of deceit is sweet to a man; but afterwards his mouth shall be filled with gravel" (Proverbs 20:17)*. If our mouths become filled with gravel, surely we are partaking of the food of the enemy. Pride makes you susceptible to deception. God will send people to warn us and save us from deception, BUT only if we in humility receive the warning. We need to humble ourselves to be taught by the Spirit of God, even if it is through others whom God has sent.

King Saul, the first King of Israel, fell into the trap of self-deception because of pride, by trying to justify his disobedient actions, which ultimately led to his ruin. The prophet reminded him how God had exalted him when he was humble.

> *And Samuel said, When thou wast little in thine own sight, wast thou not made the head of the tribes of Israel, and the Lord anointed thee king over Israel? (1 Samuel 15: 17).*

May we all remain little in our own eyes! The Bible warns us: *for if a man think himself to be something, when he is nothing, he deceiveth himself (Galatians 6:3)*. As I was reflecting on this story I asked of the Lord:

> *Dear Papa,*
> *Does humility lead to obedience, or does obedience lead to humility?*

He answered me:

> *Dear Child,*
> *Humility leads to obedience, for only when you humble yourself before Me will you have the grace to be obedient.*

Even My Son learned obedience through suffering. And suffering will reap humility. Learn of Him, the expression of humility.
Thus saith Papa.

Though he were a Son, yet learned he obedience by the things which he suffered (Hebrews 5:8).

I now understood that suffering from trials leads to dependence on Papa, for then I realize my weakness. When I am weak, then I am humbled to rely on His strength, which is sufficient.

And he said unto me, My grace is sufficient for thee: for my strength is made perfect in weakness. Most gladly therefore will I rather glory in my infirmities, that the power of Christ may rest upon me (2 Corinthians 12:9).

➢ Suffering will lead me to humility.

➢ Humility will lead me to obedience.

➢ Obedience will lead me to maturity.

During my spiritual walk I have come across those times when I lacked the grace to obey the commandment to forgive. I'm sure we have all been there at some time. While seeking God's help, He led me to this scripture: *yea, all of you be subject one to another, and be clothed with humility: for God resisteth the proud, and giveth grace to the humble (1 Peter 5:5).*

The Holy Spirit illuminated the root of my problem, it wasn't unforgiveness, it was pride!

The unforgiveness was only the fruit of the root. So you see, if we are humble, God will give us the grace needed to forgive or obey any of His commandments. If we lack grace it is because of pride. Truly humility will lead to obedience.

Dear Child,
Humility is the fruit of dying to self. Pride feeds self that it may survive and not die. Only in dying to self will your life produce the fruit of the Spirit. By protecting and pampering and feeding self, the only fruit produced is the fruit of the flesh. Humility is not taught nor given, can't you see it is not a gift? It is a fruit, and can only be produced by denying self. To stay humble you need to keep presenting yourself as a living sacrifice.
Thus saith Papa.

Let nothing be done through strife or vainglory; but in lowliness of mind let each esteem other better than themselves (Philippians 2:3).

The most difficult to achieve of all Christian virtues is humility and lowliness of mind. To count another better than myself is the problem. So when I consider myself I look at the 'old man' but when I consider another I look at the 'new man,' the new creation he is in Christ. I see the treasure in the earthen vessel; I see beyond the dust of fallen man in others but when I look at myself I remember I am dust. The Scottish poet Robert Burns penned a provoking line along this thought: "Oh that God would give us the gift to see ourselves as others see us! It would from many a blunder free us."[29]

For by the grace given to me I say to everyone among you not to think of yourself more highly than you ought to think, but to think with sober judgment (Romans 12:3).

When the Lord Jesus entered Jerusalem riding on a colt, the crowds shouted in accumulation. Let us suppose for a moment that the colt upon hearing the cry of Hosanna and seeing the branches on the road, should turn to the Lord and ask: "is this cry for you or me?" Or should turn to its mother, and say: "after all, I was the chosen one, so I'm nobler than you." It would be evident that the colt did not recognize the One who rode upon it. "Many of us who are God's servants are just as eager to be praised. The shouts of hosanna are never for us, nor are the palm branches, though we should discover them beneath our feet,"[30] states Watchman Nee.

As the colt was chosen to lift Him up on His ride to Jerusalem, we also may be chosen to lift Him up on our way to the heavenly Jerusalem. However let us always remember we are being USED by God's sovereign grace and choice to LIFT HIM UP!

For who maketh thee to differ from another? And what hast thou that thou didst not receive? Now if thou didst receive it, why dost thou glory, as if thou hadst not received it? (1 Corinthians 4:7).

As Andrew Murray states in his book on Humility: "self-condemnation is not the secret to humility. It is not sin that humbles us most but

---

[29] 'To A Louse', poem by Robert Burns, 1786.
[30] Watchman Nee, *op. cit.*, Devotion April 5.

grace. When we see that humility is something infinitely deeper than contrition, and accept it as our participation in the life of Jesus, we will begin to learn that humility is true nobility. We will begin to understand that being servants of all is the highest fulfillment of our destiny, as men created in the image of God."[31]

> *But he that is greatest among you shall be your servant. And whosoever shall exalt himself shall be abased; and he that shall humble himself shall be exalted (Matthew 23:11-12).*

Self-condemnation is often a form of self-pity. And anything with self stems from the old nature of pride.

Humility is not being beaten down. Humility is not weakness.

Humility is not passive but active because it is voluntary surrender realizing our total dependence upon God. It is a heart bowed before God and not necessarily a physical position. A body can bow down without an unbent heart on the inside. I am reminded of a story of a rebellious young child who insisted on standing up in the car instead of sitting down. When his parents demanded that he sit down, he did so reluctantly saying "I may be sitting down but inside I am still standing up!" How often have we reluctantly bowed the physical knee in God's presence, while in our spirit still rebelliously standing.

Humility is not burying your talent and saying, 'I cannot'. That is certainly not humility. That is timidity and doubt masquerading in a cloak of spirituality. If we strip off the cloak we would find hidden

---

[31] Andrew Murray, *Humility*, Whitaker House, 1982, p. 6-7.

fear that believes the words of the enemy instead of faith in God's word.

> Then he which had received the one talent came and said, Lord, I knew thee that thou art an hard man, And I was afraid, and went and hid thy talent in the earth: His lord answered and said unto him, Thou wicked and slothful servant (Matthew 25:24-26).

I was struggling one day with this issue of burying my talent to appear humble or investing my talent and run the risk of appearing arrogant. So I took it to the Lord in prayer:

> *Dear Father,*
> *Develop within me a lowliness of mind and true humility that I may humbly walk before you all the days of my life. Papa, I want to walk humbly before You without burying my talent. I want to walk humbly before you without belittling my gifting. Father, this must be your working. When I feel pride surface, I try to handle it by belittling your investment in me. I know this is not true humility.*
> *Help me, Papa!*

He told me:

> *Dear Child,*
> *The flesh cannot beget anything that is of the spirit! To belittle your gifting is a form of pride, trying to manufacture a humility that you can be proud of! When you belittle your gifting you are not belittling yourself, you are belittling Me, for I am the Giver of the gift. You can only walk humbly before Me as you walk in the spirit. Remember the dust! Only the heart and trial of your faith are gold.*
> *Thus saith Papa.*

Beware of the stench of false humility which is really only pride cleaned up on the outside and yet inside the root is still festering.

Woe unto you, scribes and Pharisees, hypocrites! For ye are like unto whited sepulchres, which indeed appear beautiful outward, but are within full of dead men's bones, and of all uncleanness. Even so ye also outwardly appear righteous unto men, but within ye are full of hypocrisy and iniquity (Matthew 23:27-28).

"Humility is a grace that should genuinely move people, but the way some of us Christians parade our humility reveals plainly the falsity of our hearts. We talk endlessly of being humble, but only display thereby what Paul calls a 'voluntary humility' (Colossians 2:18) - worked up of his own mere will - having hidden motives and not the genuine article. It were really better to call it pride,"[32] writes Watchman Nee. Are we acting humble or are we humble? Humility is not something we do it is something we are!

Dear Child,
Pride is a terrible slave master! If you are meek and lowly, then you are humble and will not have to carry the burden, which pride causes by having to prove oneself. You won't need to prove anything and therefore no stressful burden trying to prove it. Just know who you are in Me! Walk in it, don't be anxious or concerned about proving who you are. Let your confidence in Our relationship be sufficient. Learn of Me for I am meek and lowly.
Thus saith the Lord Jesus.

As God's people we may erroneously think that we need a contrite spirit only when we first repent and believe in the Lord, or

---

[32] Watchman Nee, *op. cit.,* Devotion June 6.

163

when we subsequently fall into sin. But God looks for a state of contrition in us at all times. Even when we do not sin daily, we are none the less required by Him to be of a humble spirit, remembering that we have a sinful nature that may be stirred up again at any moment. We dare not trust ourselves, but acknowledge that unless sustained by God we will certainly fall. This is contrition of spirit. With this man God dwells! So often we fail to grow in true humility because we try to crucify the flesh without living unto God.

- Humility is dying to self!
- Holiness is living unto God!

Remember that humility leads to obedience, which is a fruit of holiness. We will never have the power to overcome the prideful nature of the old man until we yield our members unto righteousness. I prayed:

Dear Father,
How can I present myself as a living sacrifice, when 'living'
speaks of life and 'sacrifice' speaks of death?

He replied:

Dear Child,
It is a matter of dying to self BUT also living unto Me!
Many try to die to self without living unto Me! Thus the
struggle with the flesh.
Dying to self without living unto Me, is trying to use your
own self will to die! But that is only cutting off the fruit

without putting an axe to the root. Only when you live unto
Me is there power available to die to self.
Dying to self can become a religion without Me.
But with Me it becomes a relationship. Trying to die to self
without Me can become judgmental!
Dying to self and living unto Me becomes a vessel of grace,
mercy and humility.
Thus saith Papa.

For if we have been planted together in the likeness of his death, we shall be
also in the likeness of his resurrection: Knowing this, that our old man is
crucified with him, that the body of sin might be destroyed, that henceforth we
should not serve sin. For he that is dead is freed from sin. Now if we be dead
with Christ, we believe that we shall also live with him: Knowing that Christ
being raised from the dead dieth no more; death hath no more dominion over
him. For in that he died, he died unto sin once: but in that he liveth, he liveth
unto God. Likewise reckon ye also yourselves to be dead indeed unto sin, but
alive unto God through Jesus Christ our Lord (Romans 6:5-11).

We cannot manufacture humility because humility is not something we say or do, but rather it is something we are. We dare not press on into His presence cloaked in false humility. We must humbly stand naked before Him. As the old hymn says: "nothing in my hand I bring, simply to thy cross I cling."[33]

3. Holiness

Just as the key to praise is a heart of gratitude, and the key to His presence is a contrite, humble heart, even so the key to worship is a holy heart.

---

[33] "Rock of Ages," hymn by Rev. Augustus Montague Toplady, 1763.

Who shall ascend into the hill of the Lord? Or who shall stand in his holy place? He that hath clean hands, and a pure heart; who hath not lifted up his soul unto vanity, nor sworn deceitfully (Psalm 24:3-4).

It is amazing how many believers assume that it is optional to be holy. Saints, it is not a suggestion, it is a command of the Lord. Has He not said, *"for I am the Lord your God: ye shall therefore sanctify yourselves, and ye shall be holy; for I am holy?"(Leviticus 11:44).* Surely if the Bible warns us to *"follow peace with all men, and holiness, without which no man shall see the Lord" (Hebrews 12:14),* we must realize that we have no choice except to walk in holiness before Him. Do not be discouraged for you may be asking, "If that is the criterion, who could ever meet that expectation?" That all depends on your understanding of "holiness." Would God command something from us that is not possible? I think not, for when He gives a command He also gives the power to fulfill that command. Otherwise how could we ever be held accountable for our actions? A holy life that is pleasing to God is not a mere demand, but is the actual living power available to live that life. The Lord Jesus came into the world, not only to do the will of God, but also to enable us to do it too.

Let us first of all take a look at what holiness is not. There are two extremes when it comes to the doctrine of holiness. One is liberalism and the other is legalism. Liberalism promotes that since we are saved by grace we are free to live as we please. But the Word admonishes us: *what then? Shall we sin, because we are not under the law, but under grace? God forbid! (Romans 6:15).* Liberalism tries to be relevant to the current society whose standards are always changing. But God's Word and standards have not changed. Man's attempt to lower God's standard to match man's behavior simply does not work. Jesus is our only standard.

Looking unto Jesus the author and finisher of our faith (Romans 6:15).

Legalism on the other hand is a list of external do's and don'ts, which brings us back into bondage. If externalism were evidence of holiness, then the Lord Jesus would have considered the Pharisees holy. Yet He warns: *"for I say unto you, that except your righteousness shall exceed the righteousness of the scribes and Pharisees, ye shall in no case enter into the kingdom of heaven" (Matthew 5:20).*

Legalism is a judgmental heart dressed up in the filthy rags of self-righteousness as declared in Isaiah 64:6: *but we are all as an unclean thing, and all our righteousnesses are as filthy rags.* At the same time this judgmental heart is judging others if they are not wearing the same spiritual wardrobe of do's and don'ts: *for they being ignorant of God's righteousness, and going about to establish their own righteousness, have not submitted themselves unto the righteousness of God (Romans 10:3).*

A life of legalism is controlled by an external code of ethics but a life of holiness is controlled by the inward dwelling of Christ.

I am crucified with Christ: nevertheless I live; yet not I, but Christ liveth in me: and the life which I now live in the flesh I live by the faith of the Son of God, who loved me, and gave himself for me (Galatians 2:20).

External observances without internal piety are as nothing.

Woe unto you, scribes and Pharisees, hypocrites! For ye make clean the outside of the cup and of the platter, but within they are full of extortion and excess. Thou blind Pharisee, cleanse first that which is within the cup and platter, that the outside of them may be clean also (Matthew 23:25-26).

Holiness is voluntary submission to His will from the heart. It is the difference between "I must, I have to" and "I choose to, I delight to." One is a burden while one is a joy. A burden is resented whereas a joy is welcomed.

In legalism the flesh is looked upon as a burden and a hindrance to the spirit. Whereas in holiness the flesh is brought under submission to the spirit.

Holiness is from within but legalism is from without, with a set of rules to crucify the flesh by mere will power, e.g. like lawyers looking for loopholes in the law. How close can I sleep to the edge of the bed without falling out?

- Holiness is an inward surrender allowing His power to flow from within.
- Holiness gives liberty to live by His grace.
- Legalism is bondage trying to beat the flesh into submission.

The Greek word for holiness is *'hagiasmos'* which literally means 'to be set apart'. In the Bible it is the same word that is translated 'sanctification'. *'Hagios'* is the same root word we translate 'saints' but could also be translated 'holy ones'. Believers are always referred to as 'saints' in the Bible. Only once are they called

Christians in Acts 11:26...*And the disciples were called Christians first in Antioch.* Only twice are they referred to as believers in Acts 5:14...*And believers were the more added to the Lord.* And *let no man despise thy youth; but be thou an example of the believers, in word, in conversation, in charity, in spirit, in faith, in purity (1 Timothy 4:12).* Everywhere else they are called saints or 'holy ones'.

Why are we called the 'holy ones'? The word for sanctuary is the same root word *'hagion'* which means a holy place set apart for God. In the Old Testament the sanctuary was the Holy of Holies of the tabernacle where God dwelt with His people. But God now dwells in a sanctuary not made with hands, i.e. the body of the saint, making him a 'holy one', because his body is now a 'holy place' where God dwells by His spirit.

> *Know ye not that ye are the temple of God, and that the Spirit of God dwelleth in you? (1 Corinthians 3:16). What? Know ye not that your body is the temple of the Holy Ghost which is in you, which ye have of God, and ye are not your own? For ye are bought with a price: therefore glorify God in your body, and in your spirit, which are God's (1 Corinthians 6:19-20).*

Why are we called the "holy ones? Because the Holy One dwells in our inner most being. Therefore we are only saints because we are also a sanctuary.

> *And he charged them, saying, Thus shall ye do in the fear of the Lord, faithfully, and with a perfect heart (2 Chronicles 19:9).*

"We must see to it that we act from a good principle; we must do all in the fear of the Lord, setting Him always before us, and then we would act faithfully and conscientiously, and with a perfect, upright heart,"[34] says Matthew Henry.

If we have a desire to press into God's presence we must come with a holy heart according to the Word which tells us *"without holiness no man shall see the* Lord" (Hebrews 12:14). How then can a holy heart be produced in fallen man? The answer is in the following scripture:

> *Having therefore these promises, dearly beloved, let us cleanse ourselves from all filthiness of the flesh and spirit, perfecting holiness in the fear of God (2 Corinthians 7:1).*

While I was digesting this scripture I prayed:

> *Dear Papa,*
> *Work in my heart that I may always have a reverent fear that it might direct the motives and attitudes of my heart. Thank you for the blood that broke down the partition that I may come to You. God forbid that I would build other partitions in my heart and shut you out because of actions and attitudes that are displeasing to You.*

He replied:

> *Dear Child,*
> *If you truly fear Me it will set you free, not punish you, because that fear will give you the courage to let go, the motivation to walk away from that which holds you in bondage. It is sin that is the slave master, not the fear of my presence and facing me as you come to fellowship with me. As you reverently fear me, Child, you will walk uprightly and have no reason to lack boldness to come into my presence.*
> *Thus saith Papa.*

---

[34] Matthew Henry, *op. cit.,* Volume 2, page 965.

The fear of God is the motivation to cause us to change our ways!

The fear of the Lord is a fountain of life, to depart from the snares of death (Proverbs 14:27).

Be not wise in thine own eyes: fear the Lord, and depart from evil (Proverbs 3:7).

The fear of the Lord is the beginning of knowledge: but fools despise wisdom and instruction (Proverbs 1:7).

In our politically correct world we have lost the principle of accountability. It is always someone else's fault. Consequently we have a very immature society with no fear of consequences. Without a responsibility for our actions we will never grow up. This is not a principle of our Heavenly Father who wants His children to mature. The Word tells us that we will reap whatever we sow. But our society has gotten to the point where we want someone else to reap what we have sown. In other words let another take the responsibility of our actions. We have tried to annul God's method of maturing His children. God has a lot of childish adults in His Body, when He is looking for adult children.

We will never mature without learning from our mistakes, and we will never learn from those mistakes if we do not take responsibility, and we will never take responsibility without fear of consequences. Unfortunately this philosophy has crept into many of our churches, where many have lost a fear and respect for God. Surely this is also true in our society in general, where we see children growing up with no fear or respect for parents, no fear or respect for teachers and no fear or respect for the law or any authority. Where we find a lack of the fear of God we also find a lack of holiness, because the Word clearly tells us to

"Perfect holiness in the fear of God" (2 Corinthians 7:1). The Greek word for fear in this verse is *'phobos'*. It means 'terror or dread', where we get our English word *'phobia'*. Vine's expository dictionary explains it this way: "Fear of God is a controlling motive of life, in spiritual and moral matters, not a mere fear of His power and righteous retribution, but a wholesome dread of displeasing Him, a fear that will banish the terror that shrinks from His presence. It will inspire a constant carefulness in dealing with others."

Some may question: "but wouldn't that fear rob me of my joy which is my strength?" I asked the Lord the same question:

Dear Father,
May warnings from Your Word stir up a fear that will lead me to grow in holiness and righteousness. But can the "Joy of the Lord" and the "Fear of God" abide in the same heart?

This was His answer:

Dear Child,
The 'Fear of God' is the guard of the heart, lest you fall away.
If you fall away the joy will be gone.
The 'Joy of the Lord' is the fruit of walking with Me and having a guiltless relationship with Me.
The 'Fear of God' will guard that precious relationship.

*The 'Fear of God' protects the 'Joy of the Lord' because the
fear motivates the guiltless relationship. The 'Joy of the Lord'
is the result of that relationship.*
Thus saith Papa.

What is holiness?

➢ Holiness is to have a perfect heart.

What is a perfect heart?

➢ A perfect heart is a willing heart.

What is a willing heart?

➢ A heart that is willing to be broken.
➢ A heart that is willing to be molded.
➢ A heart that bows to His Lordship.

As Thomas Merton, an Anglo-American Catholic writer and
Trappist monk wrote in his journal: "My Lord God, I believe that the
desire to please you does in fact please you."[35]

Dear Child,
Many desire My presence but for the wrong reason!
They want power without the cleansing!
They want the anointing without the holiness!
*They seek soulish satisfaction without total surrender to the
Spirit. Without total surrender to the Spirit they cannot
conceive the fruit of the spirit.*
Thus saith Papa.

---

[35] Thomas Merton, *Thoughts in Solitude*, Farra, Straus and Giroux, New York,
1956.

As we prepare to press on into His presence may we strip our hearts of the leaves of self-sufficiency, false humility and self-righteousness. As we stand before Him totally naked, clothed only in gratitude, humility and holiness do we have a heart that is bowed to His Lordship.

> *Oh that we might know the Lord! Let us press on to know Him, and He will respond to us as surely as the coming of the dawn or the rain of early spring (Hosea 6:3 - Living Bible translation).*

CHAPTER TEN

CHANGED FROM GLORY TO GLORY

*But we all, with open face beholding as in a glass the glory of the
Lord, are changed into the same image from glory to glory, even
as by the Spirit of the Lord (2 Corinthians 3:18).*

The purpose of developing a secret history with God is to cultivate a healthy spiritual root structure. It is only with this deep root
structure that we will be able to survive the heat of testings and
trials in our lives. And it is only through these testings and trials we
will mature in the faith as we exercise our spiritual muscles. If our
root structure is shallow we will wither away by the scorch of the
trials like those in the parable of the sower.

*Some fell upon stony places, where they had not much earth: and forthwith
they sprung up, because they had no deepness of earth: And when the sun was
up, they were scorched; and because they had no root, they withered away
(Matthew 13:5).*

Our root structure is an allegory of our unseen life, which is our
character, because our character is who we are while nobody is
looking. If we desire to grow up in the faith, our character must
ripen to the maturity of the fruit of the spirit. It will only ripen to the
fruit of the spirit as we develop deep healthy roots. If the roots of
our character are deeply grounded in the True Vine, we will not be

moved when the heat of trials tests our faith, and we will stay true to our roots. It is in our secret time with God that our character is developed as He conforms us to His image.

In the opening scripture above the Greek for 'changed' in 2 Corinthians 3:18 is *'metamorphosis'* which literally means a change in form and a change in character especially by supernatural means. A fine example would be the unexplainable metamorphosis of a beautiful butterfly emerging from the dying shell of a caterpillar. Likewise it is in our secret time with God that we will emerge from our dying self-life to a brand new creation, a metamorphosis by the power of God. He is conforming us on the inside that the outside will bring honor to His kingdom. As we press through to the Holy of Holies where we invest time alone with our Heavenly Father, we are being changed in the inner man that we might manifest His spirit in our walk when we return to the Outer Court. So often we try to put the cart before the horse, by trying to be changed by doing instead of doing because we have been changed.

He spoke to me:

> *Dear Child,*
> *I am more concerned with what you are becoming than what you are doing! And therefore the fruit I am looking for in your life and from time spent with Me is character, growth and the fruit of My Spirit. As your spiritual roots are developed you will bear the fruit of the roots. Then when you*

176

lay down your life for others the seed from the fruit of your life will in due season bear the same fruit in the lives of others. Thus My Kingdom will grow!

The fruit of your life must contain spiritual seeds if they are to give life to others. Spiritual seeds can only be conceived in your time of intimacy with Me, lest you are only tickling ears, that bear the fruit of the flesh that can only satisfy the emotional soul man and not the spirit man.

Thus saith Papa.

We learn the lesson He is teaching us in the Holy Place after our inward man, but we live out the lesson through our actions in our outward man when we walk in the Outer Court.

The Holy Place is where we 'BECOME' and the Outer Court is where we 'DO'.

We need to invest in the ROOT STRUCTURE and the HARVEST will bring glory to God.

We must take care of what our eyes see or our ears hear, for it has been said that we become what we behold. Are we allowing the world to pour us into its mold, by giving into peer pressure from our friends or the standards of our culture? Or are we yielding to the Holy Spirit that He might mold us? *And be not conformed to this world: but be ye transformed by the renewing of your mind (Romans 12:2).* If our destiny is to be conformed to His image as according to Romans 8:29, *for whom he did foreknow, he also did predestinate to be conformed to the image of his Son;* we need to invest more time in developing our relationship with the Father, that we may behold more and more of His character, His heart and His mind.

> *Yet a little while, and the world seeth me no more; but ye see me: because I live, ye shall live also. He that hath my commandments, and keepeth them, he it is that loveth me: and he that loveth me shall be loved of my Father, and I will love him, and will manifest myself to him (John 14:19-21).*

After His resurrection, the Lord Jesus could not be seen in the world after the flesh. Only those who are born of His spirit can see Him in the spiritual realm and through the eyes of the spirit. As we walk in obedience to His word, He will show Himself to us. The more our eyes are illuminated to see God and His holiness, the more we will see ourselves in our shortcomings, and will have a desire to yield that He may change us. "He who has glimpsed the blaze of God's light has seen himself, too, as he really is,"[36] states Watchman Nee.

Being born again takes a moment but maturity takes a lifetime. A weed may sprout up overnight, but quickly wilts in the heat and drought because it does not have deep roots to nourish and water it. In the time of drought, the healthy roots of a plant or tree, will grow down deeper in search of water in the depth of the earth.

The Lord told me:

> *Dear Child,*
> *Study what the drought and the scorches of the sun have done to your garden and learn a parable. See your roses, the root is striving to produce, that is its purpose, but see how*

---

[36] Watchman Nee, *op. cit.*, Devotion March 14.

small the roses are and how they lack their normal fragrance. It is almost as if the potential bud does not fully develop and almost dies on the vine. See how the trees that do not have deep roots wither and die when a drought comes. The trees with deep roots survive from the hidden water deep in the earth. Spiritually this is how you will survive during a time of drought and heat of trials. You will be nourished from the hidden manna of your deep roots and secret history with Me, and the fruit your life will bear will be the fruit that will be everlasting and a sweet fragrance to Me.

As you dedicate this time with Me the flower that will be produced from your life will not be a disappointment. It will not die on the vine because you are nourishing it daily with your time alone with Me.

Thus saith Papa.

I have often wondered why I needed to pray for something when according to the Word, He already knows before I ask, *"be not ye therefore like unto them: for your Father knoweth what things ye have need of, before ye ask him" (Matthew 6:8).* Then I realized that I need to pray in order that I might be changed. Our prayer time is more about changing and maturing us than having our needs met.

As I was meditating on the story from Mark 5:25-34, about the woman who touched the hem of His garment, I offered this prayer:

Dear Father,
You are such a caring, loving Papa, and you know each time one of your children reaches out in faith to touch You! Father, I don't want to be one of the throng, I want to daily reach out and touch You, see You more clearly, and hear

your heartbeat. All this I am doing in faith! Papa, honor that small grain of faith, that I may experience Your touch and fellowship.

He encouraged me :

Dear Child,
You will experience that touch daily as I touch and mold you to My image, as I heal you of your old self. You will know as I pour My spirit in that mold, My power and My virtue into that mold, for you no longer live but I live in you! As you reach out in faith and sincerity of heart, the virtue will flow from My Father's heart to My child's heart, that My charac-ter and likeness will be formed in that heart. Nothing in the throng is hid from My sight. I know all the contents of the heart, and I know those who touch Me in faith and sincerity. I am touched by the faithful cry of a sincere heart. A sincere heart, is a heart that is naked before Me, honest with self and honest with Me, not trying to cover with rags of self-righteousness, surrendering the will and independence of self, and confessing dependence on My grace alone.
Thus saith Papa.

May we all pray: "Father, Cover my naked heart with your grace and garment of your righteousness alone!" We are changed from glory to glory as we daily visit the Potter's house. As we yield to the work of His Hand, the Great Potter will mold the clay of our lives into a vessel that is pleasing to Him.

Arise, and go down to the potter's house, and there I will cause thee to hear my words. Then I went down to the potter's house, and, behold, he wrought a work on the wheels. And the vessel that he made of clay was marred in the hand of the potter: so he made it again another vessel, as seemed good to the potter to make it (Jeremiah 18: 2-4).

Although we were only formed out of clay, He created us in His image, but that image has been defaced because of sin.

So God created man in his own image, in the image of God created he him; male and female created he them (Genesis 1:27). And the Lord God formed man of the dust of the ground, and breathed into his nostrils the breath of life; and man became a living soul (Genesis 2:7).

Jeremiah tells us how the Potter takes the clay that was marred, and makes it into another vessel, that will once again bear an image that will glorify the Creator.

One radiant autumn morning as the sun blazed the landscape with fiery vibrant colors, I paused to offer this prayer:

Dear Father,
Your creation is so beautiful and awe inspiring in all seasons, oh Papa, that the new life You are creating in me, would also be so inspiring throughout all seasons of my life!

He answered me:

Dear Child,
As nature brings glory to My Name, I also desire My children to bring glory to My Name. All creation was spoken into existence but man was created, man was formed from a mold. He was formed in My Image! I am remolding you daily on My wheel at the potter's shed. Yield and be obedient. Thus saith Papa.

How does the Potter mold us to that image? He molds us through His Word during our time alone with Him. The WORD is the Potter's wheel. We must allow it to mold and transform us. If we are not IN the WORD we are not on the wheel. Do we yield that it might transform us or do we jump off the wheel without it making a molding impact on our hearts? By listening we have visited the Potter's shed! But only as we act upon that which we have heard, have we been on the wheel! Only when our actions change have we been molded.

One day I had a problem with my printer, and although it went through all the motions, it didn't print the words, there was only a blank page. God used this as a window to my soul and spoke this parable to my heart:

> *Dear Child,*
> *Am I only an impression on your life or is there an imprint on your life when you leave My presence. Is your life only a blank page that has gone through the motions but no lasting imprint? Live what I impress upon your heart, and it will be read of men. As you live what I impress upon your heart, your life will be anointed with the indelible ink of the Holy Spirit to make an imprint on the hearts of others.*
> *Thus saith Papa.*

When we spend time alone in God's presence, others will know that we have been changed by the authenticity and integrity of our walk. As the priest of Israel spent time alone with God in the Holy

Place, he would burn incense as he ministered unto God at the Golden Altar of Incense. When he left the Holy Place and came out to the Outer Court, the people would know that he had been in God's presence, because they could smell the incense on his robes. Do others smell that incense as we walk in the world after leaving His presence? Are we outliving the inliving?

Ye are our epistle written in our hearts, known and read of all men: Forasmuch as ye are manifestly declared to be the epistle of Christ ministered by us, written not with ink, but with the Spirit of the living God; not in tables of stone, but in fleshly tables of the heart (2 Corinthians 2:2-3).

How can the Potter's wheel, which is an allegory of the Word, change us? The Lord clarified it:

Dear Child,
My word is sharp and powerful like a two-edged sword, to the cutting asunder of soul and spirit. Only My Word can bring light and so distinguish between that which is soulish and that which is spiritual! A word from Me will bring that light, no gray, a quick sharp cut; this is black or this is white. It is time for My children to grow up and learn discernment, lest they be deceived by the works of the soulish man, instead of the works of the spirit!
Thus saith Papa.

For the word of God is quick, and powerful, and sharper than any two-edged sword, piercing even to the dividing asunder of soul and spirit, and of the joints and marrow, and is a discerner of the thoughts and intents of the heart (Hebrews 4:12).

And he had in his right hand seven stars: and out of his mouth went a sharp two-edged sword: and his countenance was as the sun shineth in his strength (Revelation 1:16).

Whether through the written Word, or a word spoken to our hearts, or even a word through a window to our souls, that word is a two-edged sword that has the power to change us:

> *Dear Child,*
> *Be still on the potter's wheel that I may mold you daily into a vessel that is pleasing to Me, with My signature, because daily I am transforming you into My likeness, and you are My creation. Your life will then have My seal and stamp of approval, you will need no other approval! As your life honors Me, it will bring glory to the Creator, whose seal and stamp you carry. You were purchased with an awesome price, walk worthy of that cost and the investment I have made in you.*
> *Thus saith Papa.*

Nevertheless the foundation of God standeth sure, having this seal, The Lord knoweth them that are his. And, Let every one that nameth the name of Christ depart from iniquity. If a man therefore purge himself from these, he shall be a vessel unto honour, sanctified, and meet for the master's use, and prepared unto every good work (2 Timothy 2:19-21).

We are changed as we daily *"present your bodies as a living sacrifice, holy, acceptable unto God, which is your reasonable service. And be not conformed to this world: but be ye transformed by the renewing of your mind, that ye may prove what is that good, and acceptable, and perfect, will of God" (Romans 12:1-2).* In order to present this sacrifice, we must press in through the noisy bustle of the Outer Court to the quiet stillness of the Holy

Place, where we may present ourselves as a living sacrifice on the Golden Altar of Incense. The only altar in the Outer Court was the Brazen Altar where the many types of the Lamb of God were sacrificed for the sins of the people. Brass in typology always speaks of judgment. There is only One who was found worthy to be judged for the sins of the world on the Brazen Altar, that One was the spotless Lamb of God. We do not present our living sacrifices on the Brazen Altar, because He took our place on that altar in the Outer Court, which is a type of the world. The Brazen Altar speaks of separation from God, but the Golden Altar speaks of fellowship with God. When our Lamb cried out: *"My God, my God, why hast thou forsaken me?" (Matthew 27:46).* The separation He experienced, because of judgment for our sins, gives us the privilege to press through to fellowship at the Golden Altar of Incense. We cannot present ourselves at the Brazen Altar, for it is a debt we could never pay.

How can this daily pilgrimage to the Golden Altar of Incense change us? As we present ourselves daily as living sacrifices, something in us dies, to be replaced by a living piece of His Image. *For which cause we faint not; but though our outward man perish, yet the inward man is renewed day by day (2 Corinthians 4:16).* The blood He shed on the Brazen Altar made it possible for us to exchange the dying old self for His newness of life.

Dear Child,

Present your body as a living sacrifice, holy and acceptable in My sight. As every offering must be sprinkled with salt, even so your sacrifice of self must also be sprinkled with salt, which will heal and purify your life that it will be acceptable in My sight. The salt will cause a thirst for more of Me, which cannot be quenched, by only reading the Word, but by obeying it. As you obey the Word, you are drinking it and it is refreshing your thirsty soul. As you drink of this water, I am increasing in your life and the old you is decreasing. Let Me arise in power in your life and the enemies of your soul will be scattered. I salt to cause a thirst, but I also provide living water to quench that thirst. As you drink you are yielding, and as you yield, your living sacrifice is acceptable in My sight.

Thus saith Papa (see Leviticus 2:13 and Mark 9:49).

This we do every day as we approach the Golden Altar of Incense, where He increases and we decrease, during those solitary moments we spend in His presence as He searches our hearts. As we yield and obey to that which He reveals, our obedience becomes the sweet fragrant incense that seeps through the veil into the Holy of Holies This obedience is holy and acceptable to Him.

And Samuel said, Hath the Lord as great delight in burnt offerings and sacrifices, as in obeying the voice of the Lord? Behold, to obey is better than sacrifice, and to hearken than the fat of rams (1 Samuel 15:22).

Without the shedding of blood there is no remission of sin, so the only place for forgiveness is the Brazen Altar. The Golden Altar of Incense is not the place of forgiveness, it is the place of obedience.

The Brazen Altar portrays His work as our Savior, but the Golden Altar of Incense portrays our obedience to His Lordship. I said:

Dear Father,
Help me to understand 'laying down my all' on the altar,
that I may walk in Your power and might. As I offer my life
as a living sacrifice, I want it to be holy and acceptable to
You, that the fire from heaven may fall, for only then will I
know that my sacrifice is acceptable to You. Help me that it
might be a sweet savor to You, Papa.

He answered me:

Dear Child,
Sacrifice has cost! Something must die! Self must die! The
flesh must die!
Present your whole being on the altar and My fire will con-
sume that which is of the old man, and that living sacrifice
which remains will burn with power but not be consumed
and will be a sweet savor to Me.
Obedience to Me is a sweet savor.
Obedience born out of love for Me is a sweet savor.
Obedience to Me will nourish the spirit and starve the flesh.
Lose your soul life that you may have everlasting life in the
spirit.
Thus saith Papa.

We do not grow up overnight as a weed does, there is no instant maturity, but we mature daily as we develop a secret history with God, where our roots are nourished and deepened. Becoming a believer will cost you nothing but becoming a mature disciple may cost you everything, since *whosoever doth not bear his cross, and come after me, cannot be my disciple. For which of you, intending to build a tower, sitteth not down first, and counteth the cost, whether he have sufficient to finish it? Lest haply, after he hath laid the foundation, and is not able to finish it, all that behold it begin to mock him, Saying, This man began to build, and was not able to finish (Luke 14:27-30).* There is no painless path to maturity, the flesh must be crucified by daily taking up the cross. We will never learn obedience without daily taking up our cross. We will never mature without obedience. We will never be conformed to His image without maturity:

> *Dear Child,*
> *To lose life in the flesh, is to find life in the spirit.*
> *The cross is self-denial, and doing that which I have ordained you for; the cross is the key to obedience; obedience is the key to maturity; maturity is the key to conformity to the image of My Son.*
> *Take up the cross for the cross is the way to death of the flesh. Don't try to save that which satisfies the flesh for if it is starved it will die. If it dies you will find spiritual resurrection and power.*
> *Thus saith Papa.*

And he said to them all, If any man will come after me, let him deny himself, and take up his cross daily, and follow me (Luke 9:23).

Though he were a Son, yet learned he obedience by the things which he suffered... And being made perfect, he became the author of eternal salvation unto all them that obey him (Hebrews 5:8 -9).

Dear Child,

As I mold, I am restoring that which was lost in the fall. As I mold I am working on the heart, for the fall was a matter of the heart, which caused the ultimate perdition of the mind and death of the body.

The heart (spirit) is restored.

The mind (soul) is being restored.

The body will be restored.

The spirit which was dead, is made alive by My presence, when I put up My residence there, I bring light to spiritual darkness.

Disobedience and self-will quenched the light and man sat in darkness. Do not quench or grieve My spirit which dwells in you, if I am Lord, do as I ask.

Thus saith Papa.

We are triune beings with body, soul and spirit. *And the very God of peace sanctify you wholly; and I pray God your whole spirit and soul and body be preserved blameless unto the coming of our Lord Jesus Christ (1 Thessalonians 5:23).* When we are born again of His Spirit, we are new creatures: *therefore if any man be in Christ, he is a new creature: old things are passed away; behold, all things are become new (2 Corinthians 5: 17).* Yes, all things are made new but not instantly, only the spirit is new in the moment we are born of His Spirit. Yet we can look forward in faith to the day when we will have a new glorified body at the resurrection.

Who shall change our vile body, that it may be fashioned like unto his glorious body (Philippians 3:21). In a moment, in the twinkling of an eye, at the last trump: for the trumpet shall sound, and the dead shall be raised incorruptible, and we shall be changed (1 Corinthians 15:52).

However the progressive new change we are studying in this chapter is the metamorphosis of the soul, which is the seat of the mind, thoughts, the will, emotions, attitudes and motivations, which by His Spirit will be brought under the control of our new spirits.

And be not conformed to this world: but be ye transformed by the renewing of your mind, that ye may prove what is that good, and acceptable, and perfect, will of God (Romans 12:2).

Let us be careful of boasting about the sincerity of our hearts, while being careless concerning our thought life. Transformation depends on the renewing of the mind.

But I fear, lest by any means, as the serpent beguiled Eve through his subtilty, so your minds should be corrupted from the simplicity that is in Christ (2 Corinthians 11:3).

Remember and be warned that Eve's heart was still sinless at the time she allowed her thoughts to be distorted by Satan's craftiness.

Our physical birth is an event but our growing up is a process. Likewise our new birth is an event but spiritual maturity is a process. Any process takes patience. Being changed and matured does not happen overnight, but rather with consistency and perseverance in our time alone with God, little by little He is changing us until Christ be formed in us (Galatians 4:19).

When we purpose to develop a secret history with God in our hearts, our devotional time becomes much more than a religious ritual, but rather an exciting and challenging life changing experience with our Heavenly Papa.

*But now, O Lord, thou art our father; we are the clay, and thou our potter;
and we all are the work of thy hand (Isaiah 64:8).*

When we think of God as the sun and we are a mirror, unless we are facing the sun we cannot reflect the sun's rays. If your heart is deflected from simple devotion to God, then what comes out in your talk and walk will not reflect Him or His heart.

Until we see His reflection in our spiritual mirrors we still have a long way to go.

*Beloved, now are we the sons of God, and it doth not yet appear
what we shall be: but we know that, when he shall appear, we
shall be like him (1 John3:2).*

CHAPTER ELEVEN

MAINTAINING YOUR ROOT STRUCTURE

Abide in me, and I in you. As the branch cannot bear fruit of itself, except it abide in the vine; no more can ye, except ye abide in me (John 15:4).

Once I asked my Father:

Dear Father,
How do I maintain my root structure?

He answered:

Dear Child,

1. *By spending time in solitude and stillness, that I may nourish and water your roots.*

2. *By yielding that I may cut off at the root any sucker that is not of My Spirit.*

3. *By blooming where you are planted, and not uprooting yourself from where I have, in My sovereignty, planted you in My Body.*

4. *By consistently fertilizing the roots with reading and obeying the Word. Obedience to the Word breaks up the hardness of the soil of the heart.*

5. *By forgetting not your beginnings, and remember with gratitude and humility the day you were grafted into the true vine. Despise not small beginnings nor tread upon your historical roots, for I, in My sovereignty, placed you*

in your family line, for My purpose, for My honor, and for My glory.

6. *By daily sprinkling the roots with a dose of faith, as you believe in your communication with Me each day.*
   Thus saith Papa.

1- BY SPENDING TIME IN SOLITUDE AND STILLNESS, THAT I MAY NOURISH AND WATER YOUR ROOTS.

Commune with your own heart upon your bed, and be still (Psalm 4:4).

'Busyness' robs us not only of our peace, sanity, and quality of life, but more importantly of our time with God. The lack of peace, sanity and quality of life are only the fruit of the root problem. The root problem is our choice, to not invest time alone with God. Have you ever cried 'Stop the world I want to get off'?

What we need is to take time out and spend it in solitude and stillness in the presence of God, for in the silence of that moment, we have transcended into God's time zone and tasted eternity if only for a brief moment. With spiritual eyes we will see our concerns and our world from God's perspective. Most of my family live in Northern Ireland, and when I communicate with them, I am for those moments in their time zone, which is five hours ahead of mine. During that time on the phone I am seeing and experiencing life from their time zone and perspective. I may be just preparing to go out for the evening, but they are already preparing to go to bed.

Likewise when we spend time communicating with God, we will see the world from His time zone of eternity. Will the busyness we are involved in really matter in the light of eternity? The hands of the clock may still be ticking away, but our world will have stopped long enough to permit God to nourish and water our roots. This nourishment will divinely feed and strengthen the inner man and refresh the weary soul.

And Jesus said unto them, I am the bread of life: he that cometh to me shall never hunger (John 6:35).

But whosoever drinketh of the water that I shall give him shall never thirst; but the water that I shall give him shall be in him a well of water springing up into everlasting life (John 4:14).

In Luke chapter 10, we read about Jesus' visit to the home of Martha and Mary. Martha wanted to serve Jesus with much busyness, while Mary just wanted to be with Him. Like Martha, many of us want to serve the Lord with much busyness in the Outer Court, which becomes a snare, hindering us from pressing on into the Holy Place. We can justify our choice by saying, "I don't have time to spend with You today, God, but I am doing all this good work in the Outer Court for You!" While all the time God is beckoning us: "Child, spend time alone with Me! Come apart and sup with Me."

Behold, I stand at the door, and knock: if any man hear my voice, and open the door, I will come in to him, and will sup with him, and he with me (Revelation 3:20).

Jesus said Mary had chosen the better way. The 'better way' is not a matter of time it is a matter of choice.

In our generation we will do almost anything to avoid spending time alone. I am talking about quality time alone in stillness without any form of entertainment. I always say we cannot get to know a person without spending quality time with them. How well do you know yourself? Are you afraid to look deep inside to discover the real you? Is that perhaps why we avoid time alone motionless and listening only to silence? Maybe we need to invest some time in solitude and stillness with the One, who knows us the best and yet still loves us the most, and the Only One who has the power to change us by nourishing and watering our root structure.

Be still, and know that I am God (Psalm 46:10).

2- BY YIELDING THAT I MAY CUT OFF AT THE ROOT ANY SUCKER THAT IS NOT OF MY SPIRIT.

Every branch in me that beareth not fruit he taketh away: and every branch that beareth fruit, he purgeth it, that it may bring forth more fruit (John 15:2).

A sucker is a side shoot from the roots that does not bloom or grow on the true stem of the plant. It grows independent of the true stem, but its flowers are a mere imitation of the real flower, much smaller with no fragrance. In growing roses, suckers are often not detected until they bloom and their forgery is visible, reminding us of the Lord's words: *"by their fruits ye shall know them."*

We must yield to the husbandman of John 15, that He might cut off that sucker at the root level or it will only grow back stronger than ever. If we only cut off the flower and stem above the surface, we are really only pruning it, and encouraging it to grow even stronger. Only the Father can see and know what is not of His Spirit, in the deep, dark recesses of the soil of our hearts. We should all pray daily: *search me, O God, and know my heart: try me, and know my thoughts: And see if there be any wicked way in me, and lead me in the way everlasting (Psalm 139:23-24).*

When a rose develops a sucker it is really the rose going back to its old natural state.

Yet I had planted thee a noble vine, wholly a right seed: how then art thou turned into the degenerate plant of a strange vine unto me? (Jeremiah 2:21).

Suckers in our lives are signs that 'the old man' is surfacing again, and we want to produce fruit independent of the True Vine into which we were grafted (see Romans 11:17).

We are not discussing here obvious sins of the flesh; it is something much more subtle, therefore much more dangerous. Not manifested outward sins like murder or adultery, but hidden attitudes of the flesh, like self-righteousness or spiritual pride masquerading itself as manufactured humility. Remember this fruit is an imitation, therefore in some ways it is similar to the real thing. This sucker, if left to flourish, will bear a harvest of self-righteousness and spiritual pride because it has struggled and labored to produce a counterfeit fruit of the spirit apart from the True Vine.

"For apart from Me you can do nothing" (John 15:5).

3- BY BLOOMING WHERE YOU ARE PLANTED, AND NOT UPROOTING YOURSELF FROM WHERE I HAVE, IN MY SOVEREIGNTY, PLANTED YOU IN MY BODY.

But now hath God set the members every one of them in the body,
as it hath pleased him (1 Corinthians 12:18).

Many are on a 'Mission Impossible' in search of the perfect church. All I can say is, if you find it, don't join it, for then it will no longer be perfect! The church is made up of imperfect people, sinners forgiven by the grace of God. Yet many of us continue on this 'merry go round' of church hopping, in search of the kind of worship we like, the teaching we need, the fellowship we want etc. and all the time it is really all about where He wants us to be. The best church for us, is the church where He plants us. As we are hopping on and off the 'merry go round' we are pulling up our roots and harming our root structure. Deep, healthy roots only develop over a period of time planted in the same place. Shallow roots are the product of an inconsistent walk and lack of commitment to a local body, belonging to people who change churches as often as the latest season's fashion. Not only are the roots shallow, but the roots often lay bare, because it is a long period of time before they get plugged into another church. Any plant that has its roots exposed, especially to the heat of the sun, will eventually shrivel up and die. A person with shallow roots or roots laid bare may not survive spiritually once the heat of trials tries their faith.

> *Some fell upon stony places, where they had not much earth: and forthwith they sprung up, because they had no deepness of earth: And when the sun was up, they were scorched; and because they had no root, they withered away (Matthew 13:5-6).*

This does not necessarily mean that a certain local church is a life time commitment. In His timing, God may choose to transplant us. But remember only He is the True Husbandman.

> *I am the true vine, and my Father is the husbandman (John 15:1).*

Only He knows how to transplant us safely without harm to our root structure. When God digs us up to plant us in another church in His vineyard, He will do so without disturbing the root structure of others. If we uproot ourselves, especially if we are in leadership roles, it will disturb the plantings of others close to us, particularly the tender roots of young believers.

When the Lord releases us to move from our current local body, it will never be by the way of a soulish impulse or offense. We will have peace in our spirits about it, not confusion out of a soulish reaction that satisfies the flesh but quenches the spirit. In walking away because of an offense, we may be winning a battle in the flesh, but we will be losing in the spirit. To gain a victory in the spirit we must have a defeat in the flesh. In the physical realm we may think we have lost, but in the reality of the spirit realm we have won a great victory by surrendering to the spirit. In Genesis 32, we read of Jacob's wrestle with God. Jacob surrenders after God touches the hallow of his thigh. Now this may have looked like a defeat in the physical realm but God declares: *thy name shall be called no more Jacob, but Israel: for as a prince hast thou power with God and with men, and hast prevailed (Genesis 32:28).* So in losing in the flesh, Jacob actually won in the spiritual realm.

Do not allow an offense to rob you of a spiritual victory, but rather deny the emotional heat of the flesh and mature in the Lord. *Great peace have they which love thy law: and nothing shall offend them (Psalm 119:165).* In the timetable of prophecy in which we live, saints, we must grow up and learn to respond correctly to offenses, because they will never go away, they may even increase in the last days according to this Scripture: *and then shall many be offended, and shall betray one another, and shall hate one another (Matthew 24:10).*

The word for offense is *'skandalon'* and the original meaning is the part of a trap to which the bait is attached and therefore a SNARE! So recognize the enemy at work for we are not ignorant of his devices.

To whom ye forgive any thing, I forgive also: for if I forgave any thing, to whom I forgave it, for your sakes forgave I it in the person of Christ; Lest Satan should get an advantage of us: for we are not ignorant of his devices (2 Corinthians 2:10 -11).

Do not touch the bait! Do not even go there! Or the enemy will have us trapped in his snare. It is not necessarily what others do to us that hurts us the most, it is our response to those hurts. Through God's grace you have the power to choose that response. Chasing after a poisonous snake that bites us will only drive the poison through our entire system. It is far better to take measures immediately to get the poison out.

The Word tells us how to deal with offense: *moreover if thy brother shall trespass against thee, go and tell him his fault between thee and him alone: if he shall hear thee, thou hast gained thy brother. But if he will not hear thee, then take with thee one or two more, that in the mouth of two or three witnesses every word may be established (Matthew18:15-16).*

Do not build offenses on assumptions. Go to your sister or brother, as the Word says, and you may find it was only a misunderstanding. It is exceedingly ugly in the sight of the Lord for the forgiven sinner to be merciless, and the recipient of divine grace to be ungracious. Be proactive and choose now that you will respond in the biblical way, then you will not react in the heat of the moment and in the flesh, and grab the bait of the enemy. Don't be trapped, grow up instead!

This doesn't mean the offender will not be held accountable. We could use Joseph's life as a fine example. When faced with the opportunity of sweet fleshly revenge on the brothers, who had so cruelly betrayed him, he instead chose to respond and grow in the spirit and see it through God's perspective.

And Joseph said unto them, Fear not: for am I in the place of God? But as for you, ye thought evil against me; but God meant it unto good, to bring to pass, as it is this day, to save much people alive (Genesis 50:19-21).

You will only be held accountable for your response.

My daughter Angela has written a thought on this subject, which I think is very appropriate at this point. She writes:

We have gotten to the point in our society where all relationships are disposable (whether it be personal, work, family, or church). Whenever a situation arises that we don't like or doesn't happen to meet our expectations we choose to 'opt out' of the relationship. The consequences of this choice are devastating to our families, churches and communities. We have seemed to have lost the ability or desire to work through problems - confronting wrongs, admitting our own faults, covering each other in love; it appears to take too much energy. It is much easier to close the pages of one relationship and open the new and exciting pages of another one. The saddest result of this situation is the disappearing of depth in our society. When we choose to cut off relationships we also cut off the root of history we developed during the years of that relationship. We are left with shallow and superficial relationships that leave us yearning for a depth of intimacy we never seem able to attain.

I believe this is the reason why God established families. Without the structure of family, our experience on earth would be one of ever revolving relationships. But you cannot escape a family relationship the way you can other relationships. Your mother will always be your mother and your sisters will always be your sisters... There is nothing you can do to change that. All other relationships should find wisdom in the God ordained structure of the family unit.

The Lord advised me on that too:

Dear Child,
A deep relationship is not the result of a relationship without problems and offenses, but is one which overcomes problems and offenses and matures because your spiritual muscles are being exercised as you respond to one another.
The working out of problems causes the roots to grow deeper together and your history with the other person grows deeper and less shallow. You exercise your spiritual muscles by obedience to the Word and the Spirit. As you work out those lessons, I am giving you the opportunity to learn as you fellowship with other believers in The Holy Place.
Thus saith Papa.

Iron sharpeneth iron; so a man sharpeneth the countenance of his friend (Proverbs 27:17).

That is why I believe that a church is only as strong as the families in that church. The church body needs to learn the importance of family unity, for after all we are all brothers and sisters in Christ with the same Father. We must develop meaningful deep relationships within the Body that we may grow.

In his first letter to the church at Corinth, the apostle Paul refers to the mystical Body of Christ as a human body, to help us understand our need for each other and our unique and different giftings. God places us not only in a local body, but in His mystical Body as

He pleases, according to the gift He chooses to invest in each of us for the edifying of His Body.

But all these worketh that one and the selfsame Spirit, dividing to every man severally as he will (1 Corinthians 12:11).

Bloom in whatever part of the Body He places you in, if an eye be the best eye you can be, if a foot be the best foot you can be. But don't uproot yourself and try to be a hand if He has called you to be a foot!

We need to stay grounded where He has planted us, so that we may mature in the faith as we develop deep roots.

That we henceforth be no more children, tossed to and fro, and carried about with every wind of doctrine, by the sleight of men, and cunning craftiness, whereby they lie in wait to deceive (Ephesians 4:14).

4- BY CONSISTENTLY FERTILIZING THE ROOTS WITH READING AND OBEYING THE WORD. OBEDIENCE TO THE WORD BREAKS UP THE HARDNESS OF THE SOIL OF THE HEART.

Today if ye will hear his voice, harden not your hearts (Hebrews 4:7).

The abundance of the crop is decided at the time of fertilizing, not at the time of the harvest. The fertilizing is in preparation of the potential harvest. We fertilize our gardens that we may have an abundant and disease free crop. Likewise we fertilize the soil of our hearts with the Word that our lives may bear fruit that is abundant and disease free. A strong healthy plant is regularly and faithfully fertilized that it might be able to fight disease, ward off parasites and can even withstand a drought. Whereas a weak plant is susceptible to disease, will succumb to parasites, and at the best will only be in a survival mode during a time of drought.

I have previously mentioned the drought of 1999 (see page 77), which impacted my heart so much because of the allegories it taught about survival mode that I needed to reiterate it again. I can't emphasize enough the danger to our spiritual life if we are content to simply stay in a survival manner. Instead, we should be feeding our spiritual root structure with manna from heaven lest we become hardened. If we don't seek this spiritual manna we will eventually backslide and there will be no blossom or fruit from our lives. So I think it is worth another stroll around my rose garden during the time of that drought and take one more reflective peek through this window to your soul.

Dear Child,
Look at your rose garden! They look healthy enough yet no blossom and therefore no fragrance! Because of the lack of water and the scorch of the sun they are in survival mode, doing all they can just to stay alive.
My people stay too long in survival mode, and there is no fruit from their lives. Yes, they are spiritually alive and look and appear to be healthy, but where is the blossom and fragrance from their lives? They are not drawing near and supping with Me where I can give them rivers of living water to sustain them during all the trials of life.
Thus saith Papa.

After the blooming time of my daffodils and tulips in the spring, I cut off the dead blooms but not the leaves, for the bulb feeds on the nutrients from the leaves, and stores up food for the dark cold days of winter that the bulb may bloom again in the spring. Likewise we need to be storing the nutrients of the Word in our hearts, that during the dark winter days of our walk, we will have a resource to draw from, and remain faithful and not fall away.

Thy word have I hid in mine heart, that I might not sin against thee (Psalm 119:11).

During Israel's wandering in the wilderness, God provided them manna everyday to feed upon. They had to pick it fresh every morning, early before the heat of the sun melted it. The manna deteriorated if not eaten that same day, it could not be stored if not absorbed. What a lesson that is to us! Similarly we must feed on the nutrients of the Word every day, but only that which we swallow and absorb, can we store by hiding it in our hearts. Only while it is stored in our hearts will our manna stay fresh, as it becomes part of our very being. In the same way that a piece of physical bread becomes part of us as we swallow it, as it takes nutrients of life to every cell of our body. Our manna takes spiritual life to every fiber of our being that we may live by the Word. Only as we choose to

206

obey does the Word become alive, otherwise it is only the cold letter of the Word.

To 'ABSORB' means 'to take in and appropriate' or 'to make part of the existent whole'. The heavenly manna will often get no further than our minds, or at most be only chewed over in our mouths. If we don't appropriate it to our lives today and obey it, we haven't swallowed it. Remember IT COULD NOT BE STORED IF NOT ABSORBED.

As we recall Israel's history, we learn that God commanded a golden pot of manna to be placed in the Ark of the Covenant, to be a remembrance of His provision. Unlike the manna they picked, this manna did not deteriorate over time, because it was in the Holy of Holies where the presence of God dwelt with His people Israel. Since He is Life nothing can die in His presence. Likewise the hidden manna of our hearts is safely stored in our inner most being, which is the Holy of Holies of our temples, where God comes to dwell by His Spirit.

If ye love me keep my commandments (John 14:15).

5- BY FORGETTING NOT YOUR BEGINNINGS AND REMEMBER WITH GRATITUDE AND HUMILITY THE DAY YOU WERE GRAFTED INTO THE TRUE VINE. DESPISE NOT SMALL BEGINNINGS NOR TREAD UPON YOUR HISTORICAL ROOTS, FOR I, IN MY SOVEREIGN-

TY, PLACED YOU IN YOUR FAMILY LINE, FOR MY
PURPOSE, FOR MY HONOR, AND FOR MY GLORY.

*For whom he did foreknow, he also did predestinate to be
conformed to the image of his Son (Romans 8:29).*

In the Bible, God uses chapter after chapter devoted only to
genealogies, therefore our historical roots must be very important to
God. You are who went before you, rarely unique and yet part of all
those who went before you. Your heritage is who you are today.

God planned for generations to have the 'gene' pool He could
pull from to make you! Do not tread upon His sovereign planning,
for He knew the character, personality, abilities and talents He
would need when He drew up the blueprint for your life. Do not
belittle your ancestry because you are who went before you. Your
genes were in them. If you are trying to be someone you are not, you
are not being true to your root structure. Shakespeare said it well: "to
thine own self be true."[37]

God is saying: "Commit your talents, abilities, personality, temperament, your likes and dislikes, your IQ, and yes, even your looks,
submit all of who you are to Me, that under My Lordship, I may use
your life for My Purpose, My Honor and My Glory. If I wanted a
rose in My garden I wouldn't plant a daffodil. Be yourself! Be who I
created and planned for generations for you to be."

---

[37] William Shakespeare, *Hamlet*, Act 1 Scene 3, 1603.

I am not insinuating that our fallen man does not need to be changed. Of course it does! We are daily being transformed into the image of His Son, but that does not mean God is creating 'cookie cutter' Christians. We are all different. There never has been in all of history, two people with the same fingerprints! I am the mother of identical twin daughters and even identical twins have unique fingerprints. We are all so unique to our Father. He wants all of who we are, redeemed and set apart for His purpose.

With a grateful heart always thank God for your ancestry. But for the grace of God you could have been born on the streets of Calcutta, begging for food and chained to the slavery of Hinduism, or any third world country. Remember to whom much is given, much will be required. Keep the soil of your heart soft and pliable in the Master's hands, by continually remembering with gratitude and humility, the day He took your historical roots and lovingly grafted you into the True Vine. A complaining heart is a shallow heart where the Word cannot develop deep roots. So don't complain about your talents, personality, or even your looks, don't criticize the work of the Creator, for *I will praise thee; for I am fearfully and wonderfully made: marvellous are thy works; and that my soul knoweth right well (Psalm 139:14)*. About this, Watchman Nee states that:

> God had set Paul apart before he was born (Galatians 1:15-16).
> Even the profession he learned before his conversion was
> preplanned. God works like that. All that happened to you before

you were saved as well as after, has some definite meaning. Whatever your character and temperament, your strengths and weaknesses, all are pre-known by God and prepared by him with future service in view. There is no accident, for everything is within God's providence. Nothing comes by chance. Having been thus set apart from birth, none of us can afford to be casual or frivolous in our attitude to life. Each of us must expect to discover what God has planned for us, and in his time and way to enter into it. God does not write off as valueless our unregenerate days. He does not want us to deny the very human elements in our makeup by presenting instead a false, because unreal, front. He has a use for the persons we are and intends to use the real us, purified by the cross, and not some pretense, in his service.[38]

To that the Lord told me:

Dear Child,
Creation has no choice but to fulfill its purpose and be what it was created for. Man was given a choice, a free will and creative mind to fulfill My purpose or create his own. All I ask of you is to be what you were created to be. You can try to do that which you were not created to do. But you can never be what you were not created to be, no matter how you struggle!
Thus saith Papa.

Be true to your roots!

We all have spiritual historical roots as well as physical historical roots. God is not pleased when we belittle the orthodoxy of the past and the saints who went before us. Without them we wouldn't have the faith we have today. We are building on the foundation of their

---

[38] Watchman Nee, *op. cit.,* Devotion November 6.

faith with Jesus as the chief cornerstone. Do not tread upon those roots because in doing so we are blasting away our foundation.

Thy people also shall be all righteous: they shall inherit the land for ever, the branch of my planting, the work of my hands, that I may be glorified (Isaiah 60:21).

6.-BY SPRINKLING THE ROOTS WITH A DOSE OF FAITH, AS YOU BELIEVE IN YOUR COMMUNICATION WITH ME

But without faith it is impossible to please him: for he that cometh to God must believe that he is, and that he is a rewarder of them that diligently seek him (Hebrews 11:6).

All we do in the spiritual realm is by faith. Without faith we cannot communicate with the Father. Do we really believe that as we pray we are talking with God? Or do we only believe that we can talk to God? Do we only believe that He hears our prayer but we cannot hear from Him?

We must have faith and believe that it is possible to hear His voice!

To him the porter openeth; and the sheep hear his voice: and he calleth his own sheep by name, and leadeth them out. And when he putteth forth his own sheep, he goeth before them, and the sheep follow him: for they know his voice. And a stranger will they not follow, but will flee from him: for they know not the voice of strangers (John 10:3 -5).

If any of you lack wisdom, let him ask of God, that giveth to all men liberally, and upbraideth not; and it shall be given him. But let him ask in faith, nothing wavering. For he that wavereth is like a wave of the sea driven with the wind and tossed. For let not that man think that he shall receive any thing of the Lord (James 1:5 -7).

We must have faith in what we hear, in order to obey what we hear!

My sheep hear my voice, and I know them, and they follow me (John 10:27).

We are all given a measure of faith (Romans 12:3), and that faith will only grow as we use it.

We are bound to thank God always for you, brethren, as it is meet, because that your faith groweth exceedingly (2 Thessalonians 1:3).

That daily dose of faith is an antidote to doubt, fear and discouragement that can cause disease on the leaves of your life. If the leaves fall off and die, your life will never bear the fruit that God had planned. The leaves are the food and nutrients for the potential fruit. Don't let the potential of your calling whither on the vine because of doubt, fear or discouragement, feed it a booster dose of faith. In doing so you will be breathing life into the dying embers of your passion and calling. As we faithfully seek God every day, and invest the time just to sit and listen in faith for the voice of His Spirit who dwells within each of us, we will grow in the faith that we need to hear and know His voice. The more you fellowship and talk with someone, the more you grow accustomed to the sound of their voice, their character, and their heart. The less chance you would follow the voice of the enemy.

We grow accustomed to His voice by learning:

1. To discern His voice by spending more time alone in His presence.

2. To study His written Word to find Him and know His character. If it is not in line with the Word, then it is not in line with
   His character; if it is not in line with His character, you know
   it is the voice of a stranger!

3. To leave the Outer Court and pressing on into the Holiest
   Place where we can feel and hear His heartbeat. His voice will
   always express what is closest to His heart (see chapter on
   "How do I Hear His Voice?").

*The voice of the Lord is powerful; the voice of the LORD is full of
majesty (Psalm 29:4).*

As I conclude this chapter, pray with me, that we all may
mature to the fruit of the spirit in our lives as we continue to maintain our root structure in the True Vine.

Dear Father,
May I continue to bear the fruit of the Spirit in my life.
May I make my calling and election sure by doing those
things that evidence fruit in my life, lest my life and
knowledge of You becomes barren.

May His answer inspire you also.

Dear Child,
As blossom turns to the maturity of fruit, and the fruit
contains the seeds, so must your life turn to the maturity
of fruit or you will have no seeds to sow into the life of
others.
Blossom is admired but it cannot give life, only seed from
matured fruit can reproduce life in others. My Son's life
blossomed and matured to the fruit of obedience, even His

death on the cross, that He might sow the seed of everlasting life into the life of others.

Now, go take His life which is in you and give the seed away to others. Do not let that seed lay barren, to produce life it must be sown, and that takes the maturity of obedience.

Thus saith Papa.

But the fruit of the Spirit is love, joy, peace, longsuffering, gentleness, goodness, faith, Meekness, temperance: against such there is no law (Galatians 5:22-23).

Invest in the 'BECOMING' and the 'DOING' will glorify God!

Invest in the ROOT STRUCTURE and the HARVEST will bring glory to God!

> *That Christ may dwell in your hearts by faith; that ye, being rooted and grounded in love... May know the love of Christ, which passeth knowledge, that ye might be filled with all the fulness of God (Ephesians 3:17-19).*

CHAPTER TWELVE

PRACTICAL TIPS TO HELP YOU START YOUR JOURNEY

Remember that any journey starts with the first steps.
The steps of a good man are ordered by the Lord
(Psalm 37:23).

1. Have a specific time and place for your communion with the Lord

During the spring, summer and fall, I meet with God sitting on a swing overlooking my rose garden. It brings to life the words of the old song:

"I come to the garden alone while the dew is still on the roses,
And the voice I hear falling on my ears the Son of God discloses.
And He walks with me, and He talks to me and He tells me I am His own;
And the joy we share as we tarry there, none other has ever known."[39]

Wherever your specific place may be, that you choose to spend quality time with God, make that divine appointment each day. Since we are creatures of habit it will help to find that specific time and place that is best for our lifestyle. If it is the time and place that you are most comfortable with, you will be more likely to stay with

---

[39] Austin Miles, "In the Garden" *United Methodist Hymn Book,* Hymn 314, 1913.

it. Keep in that place your Bible, a devotional book if you use one, a journal, and even a special pen just for your journalizing.

2. Invite Him to sup with you (Revelation 3:20)

I evoke His presence as I pray in stillness that He search my naked heart and bring to remembrance anything that would prevent me from entering into His presence. If the Holy Spirit sheds a light on something, I remorsefully confess it that it might be cleansed by the Blood. With confidence I can now enter into His presence seeking spiritual insight as I meditate on my devotional for the day and the Bible chapter that applies to it. I don't want you to think you have to read a devotional reflection first, because sometimes I just go straight to the written Word, praying that the Holy Spirit will enlighten me to see Him more clearly and see myself more honestly, that I might become more like Him.

3. Express your prayer in writing to God

Then I open my heart to the Father by writing my innermost thoughts in my journal by sharing with Him the impact His Word has made on my heart, and praying it will make a lasting imprint on my life and my walk, when I leave His presence to minister and live for Him in the Outer Court of my everyday life. Remember He teaches us lessons in His presence, but we practice and learn those lessons in the opportunities He gives us in our everyday walk through our relationships with others.

4. Be still and listen.

I shut out my world, quieten my heart and just listen. I keep a separate notepad close at hand in case my mind wonders, which it often does in the silence of the moment, to responsibilities of worldly duties that I must not forget. As I jot down a reminder on the notepad, I have cleared my mind again, and can concentrate on the stillness of this precious moment alone with God.

5. Write what you hear in your spirit.

On the opposite page of my journal I start to write the first impression God places in my spirit. In faith I write it in the first person and just let it flow. I finish my writing by sealing it with "Thus saith Papa" least other voices try to steal it. It is a leap of faith as I yield my pen and hand. In faith submit your pen to the paper in the way you submit your heart to the Lord. He will not do the writing but He will write through you. It could be a word of encouragement, direction, hope, wisdom or sometimes a word of correction, chastisement or warning. Whatever the word may be, you can trust it will be for your good and for your spiritual growth.

6. Verify the word you heard.

Finally I read it through to check it with His written Word. If it is in line with the written Word and with His character (see chapter seven "How do I hear His voice?"), I say: "Thank you, Papa, for the Word you gave me today."

7. Don't let the enemy try to discourage you if you miss some days.

God loves you unconditionally and even though we are sanctified, He remembers that we are only made of dust.

As a father has compassion for his children, so the Lord has compassion for those who fear him. For he knows how we were made; he remembers that we are dust (Psalm 103: 13-14).

Beware when you begin to plan or practice a more effective prayer life, Satan will counteract it by making you busier than ever with needs and responsibilities, so that you have no time to spend with God. In the book of Exodus, while the Israelites were in Egypt, Moses and Aaron asked Pharaoh to let the people have 'timeout' to spend with God. Not only did Pharaoh refuse but he even added to their burden of tasks lest they would have time to go.

You shall no longer give the people straw to make bricks, as before; let them go and gather straw for themselves. But you shall require of them the same quantity of bricks as they have made previously; do not diminish it, for they are lazy; that is why they cry, 'Let us go and offer sacrifice to our God.' Let heavier work be laid on them; then they will labor at it and pay no attention to deceptive words (Exodus 5:7-9).

8. Don't let this become the burden of a religious act.

Even times of prayer can degenerate into legalism, just another item on our "spiritual" to do list. Prayer time can become a burden, if it becomes an obligation instead of a privilege, which was bought at an awesome price. Your quiet time should never be a religious duty but rather an exciting, loving investment in your relationship to your Heavenly Father:

> *Dear Child,*
> *I forgive you! I missed you, as you miss your children, but I love you unconditionally! Love your children in that way as you learn of Me and are conformed daily to My Image. I don't want condemnation or pressure or performance to draw you to this time, but My unfailing love for you. Remember I want you to want to spend time with Me, I don't want you to have to spend time with Me When you meet with other believers in church it is a corporate time. But this secret place is your intimate time with Me.*
> *Thus saith Papa.*

9. This is your personal time of intimacy with God.

This place of intimacy is my own personal spiritual growth time with my Heavenly Father. I don't consider this a time of selfish prayer but rather a time to uncover self and talk to God about my own heart at the most intimate level of communication which is total nakedness before Him. I set aside time in the evening for intercessory prayer for others. I set aside a topic for each night of the week, e.g. one night for my immediate family, my church family, the government or overseas mission, my friends and neighbors, etc.

10. Don't expose your root structure

Take a warning from Hezekiah who suffered loss because of his desire to show off all his precious things.

And Hezekiah was glad of them, and shewed them the house of his precious things, the silver, and the gold, and the spices, and the precious ointment, and all the house of his armour, and all that was found in his treasures: there was nothing in his house, nor in all his dominion, that Hezekiah shewed them not (Isaiah 39:2).

Then said he, What have they seen in thine house? And Hezekiah answered, All that is in mine house have they seen: there is nothing among my treasures that I have not shewed them (Isaiah 39:4).

I heard the Lord:

Dear Child,
Encourage! Encourage! Be a witness to the sweet fellowship of time spent with Me, then it will be a living word, for you have experienced it and lived it. But do not pull up all your roots and lay them bear, so much of our time is intimate. A plant does not have to have its roots pulled up to see how fruitful it is, that can be seen above the surface. If the roots are all pulled up they will be scorched by the sun. Keep most of those intimate moments hidden to protect that treasure. Do not cast your pearl before swine. In sharing, some of the intimacy is lost. Use discernment.
Thus saith Papa.

Be sensitive what you share with others and to whom you share it, because they may not understand or believe. Their unbelief may discourage you by pouring doubt on your faith that caused you to receive these words from God. Instead be encouraged, for that which is conceived in those private moments with God will be given birth openly.

ENJOY YOUR JOURNEY AS HE DRAWS YOU INTO HIS
PRESENCE WHERE YOU WILL DEVELOP
YOUR SECRET HISTORY WITH GOD.

*For he shall be as a tree planted by the waters, and that
spreadeth out her roots by the river, and shall not see when heat
cometh, but her leaf shall be green; and shall not be careful in
the year of drought, neither shall cease from yielding fruit
(Jeremiah 17:8).*

WALK WITH THE KING AND BE A BLESSING!

A six part study guide is available for
"Developing a Secret History with God."

A personal "My Secret History with God" journal is available.

BIBLIOGRAPHY

Acuff, Ron. "Turn your Radio on," lyrics.

Buchanan, Angela. *Essay,* 1997.

Burns, Robert. "To A Louse," poem by 1786.

Dante. "Inferno," Canto 3 Line 9, 14th century epic poem.

Dickens, Charles. *A Tale of Two Cities*, 1859.

Gire, Ken. *Windows of the Soul*, Volumes 2,4,5,6. Zondervan Publishing House, 1996.

Grant, Alan. "The Difference" Nittany Inspirations 2009.

Henry, Matthew. *Commentary* Volume 4, MacDonald Publishing Company, 1985.

Jones, E. Stanley. "Wasting time with God" Klaus Issler Intervarsity Press, 2001.

Loveland, Rolf & Graham, Brendan. *You Raised Me Up*.

Merton, Thomas. *Thoughts in Solitude*, Farra, Straus and Giroux, New York, 1956.

Miles, C. Austin. "In the Garden", Hymn 314, *United Methodist Hymn Book,* 1913.

Murray, Andrew. *Humility*, Springdale, PA: Whitaker House, 1982.

Nee, Watchman. "Song of Songs" Part 5, Mature Love CLC publications, 2006.

Nee, Watchman. *The Joyful Heart Daily Meditations*. Tyndale House Publishers, 1989.

Ray Ryder Jr., Johnny. *The Oak Tree*.

Shakespeare, William. *Hamlet,* Act 1 Scene 3, 1603.

Toplady, Augustus Montague (Rev.). "Rock of Ages" hymn, 1763.

Tozer, A.W. *The Pursuit of God*, Christian Publications, 1982.

Vincent, Thomas. *Westminster Shorter Catechism*, 1675.

Wordsworth, William. A quote from a Letter to His Wife, April 29, 1812.

MARGARET'S FAMILY

Left Rear: *David Estes, Kathleen Estes, Patsy Bass, Angela Buchanan, Jeff Buchanan*
Front: *Chernet Estes, Margaret Bass, John Bass, Misganaw Estes*

Thanks to you all for your support and encouragement!

A special thanks to my husband John for his computer skills, help and all the cups of tea to keep me going.